Picking Up the Pieces
Corruption and Democracy in Peru

Picking Up the Pieces
Corruption and Democracy in Peru

Nick Caistor and Susana Villarán

Practical
ACTION
PUBLISHING

L A B

Latin America Bureau
LONDON

Practical Action Publishing Ltd
25 Albert Street, Rugby, CV21 2SD, Warwickshire, UK
www.practicalactionpublishing.com

Picking Up the Pieces: Corruption and Democracy in Peru
first published 2006\Digitised 2015
1 Arnwell Street, London EC1R 1UL

The Latin America Bureau is an independent research and publishing
organisation. It works to broaden public understanding of issues of human
rights and social and economic justice in Latin America and the Caribbean.

Reprinted by Practical Action Publishing
Rugby, Warwickshire UK

ISBN 1 899365 75 3
ISBN 13 9781899365753 Paperback
ISBN Library Ebook: 9781909013377 PDF
Book DOI: https://doi.org/10.3362/ 9781909013377

Editing: Ralph Smith, Jean McNeil
Cover design: Disefto Atlantico, Buenos Aires
Photo: Corbis Argentina
Interior design and setting: Kate Kirkwood

Since 1974, Practical Action Publishing has published and disseminated books
and information in support of international development work throughout
the world. Practical Action Publishing is a trading name of Practical Action
Publishing Ltd (Company Reg. No. 1159018), the wholly owned publishing
company of Practical Action. Practical Action Publishing trades only in support
of its parent charity objectives and any profits are covenanted back to Practical
Action (Charity Reg.
No. 247257, Group VAT Registration No. 880 9924 76).

The manufacturer's authorised representative in the EU for product safety is
Lightning Source France, 1 Av. Johannes Gutenberg, 78310 Maurepas, France.
compliance@lightningsource.fr

Contents

Acknowledgements

This book grew out of our collaboration in Peru during the years 1999–2003, when we worked together to develop the human rights radio network created by the Instituto de Defensa Legal in Lima. Our thanks to Glatzer Tuesta, Silvia Granados, and all the other radio producers. This book is chiefly dedicated to them, and also to the radio journalists throughout Peru – from Radio Naylamp in Lambayeque in the north, to Radio Sicuani in Cuzco, and Radio La Voz de la Selva in Iquitos, as well as many other journalists from the 180 radio stations all around Perú who offered invaluable information about the real life of the country. Thanks also to Ernesto de la Jara, Carlos Basombrío and everyone at IDL. Also María Paz Mujica who helped us with valuable documentation, and Cristián Sánchez of the British Council in Peru (QEPD). In Britain, we thank the secretaries of the Peru Support Group, Hannah Morley and Sophie Paton for their encouragement, and John Crabtree for his considerable help. And thanks of course to our families, especially Manuel Piqueras and Amanda Hopkinson, for their interest and patience.

Abbreviations

APEC	Asia–Pacific Economic Co-operation
APRA	Alianza Peruana Revolucionaria Americana
CERIAJUS	Special Commission for the Integral Reform of the Justice System
CIA	Central Intelligence Agency
CLADEM	Centro LatinoAmericano de Desarrollo de la Mujer (Latin American Centre for Women's Development)
CLAE	(business group) (chapter 2)
COPRI	Comisión de Promoción de la Inversión Privada (Commission for the Promotion of Private Investment)
DEA	Drug Enforcement Agency
FARC	Fuerzas Armadas Revolucionarias Colombiana
FIM	Frente Independiente Moralizador
FREDEMO	Frente Democrático
IDEELE	Instituto de Defensa Legal
IPAF	Instituto Peruano de Arqueología Forense
MRTA	Movimiento Revolucionario Tupac Amaru
NGO	non-governmental organisation
OAS	Organisation of American States
PAP	Partido Aprista Peruano
PPC	Partido Popular Cristiano
PRONAA	Programa Nacional de Asistencia Alimentaria (National Food Aid Programme)
PSUC	
SIN	Servicio Nacional de Inteligencia (National Intelligence Service)
TRC	Truth and Reconciliation Commission
UNFPA	United Nations Population Fund
USAID	United States Agency for International Development

Introduction

The 2006 general elections in Peru aroused great expectations. For the first time since the early 1980s, the country was free of violence. The 16.5 million voters could choose freely between a wide range of candidates for both president and congress. The traditional parties appeared to have recovered from their eclipse during the 1990s. Incumbent president Alejandro Toledo respected the rules and timetable for the vote. New political groups, born of the experience of the struggle against all the illegitimate chicanery of the Fujimori regime, offered fresh choices to the electorate.

In the event, however, the elections showed how fragile the modern, democratic image of Peru is. As had happened in 1989–90, a complete outsider upset all the calculations of the political classes in Lima, the Peruvian capital. Whereas sixteen years earlier this figure had been a Japanese agronomist, Alberto Fujimori, taking on the establishment in the name of hard work and honesty, this time it was Ollanta Humala, a retired army colonel who had led a rebellion against Fujimori in 2000, who emerged as the political unknown offering to give a voice to all those who felt left out of Peru's political life.

In the end, the voters chose instead to elect Alan García, the head of APRA (*Alianza Popular Revolucionaria Americana*), the party with the deepest roots in the country. But Humala's UPP (*Unión por el Perú*) won most seats in the national congress, thus establishing a powerful base for him for the future. García meanwhile has to prove to Peruvians that he can offer them something different from the chaotic misrule of his first period in office, 1985–90, when the country was torn apart by internal violence, economic incompetence and political posturing that ignored the population's real needs.

Civilian regimes have been in power in this Andean country for more than a quarter of a century now (following 12 years of military rule). During this time, the elected governments have managed only to widen the gap between the political class and many sectors of civil society. The complaint most commonly heard in Peru today is that politicians look after only themselves: they make extravagant promises during their election campaigns, but once they are elected they ignore the most basic needs of the voters and their families.

The fragility of Peruvian democracy can be seen in many ways. Since 1950, there have been almost 20 years of military government, and for long periods outside that there have been states of emergency in which the military enjoyed extra powers and many individual liberties were curtailed. Of the civilian presidents, only Fernando Belaúnde Terry and Alan García in the 1980s and Francisco Toledo (2001–2006) have served full terms in office. At the same time, between 1980 and 1995, Peruvians had to face one of the world's most determined and bloodthirsty attempts to take over the state by insurgents (the *Sendero Luminoso* or Shining Path guerrilla group). In their distorted way, the Shining Path were trying to take advantage of the distance between the Andean highland peoples of Aymara or Quechua descent and the Peruvian state, with which they often came into contact only in a negative way: to be press-ganged into the armed forces, forced to pay taxes, or made to pay bribes for all kinds of permits for their everyday lives.

To illustrate this neglect of a significant part of the population, it was only with the 1979 Constitution, which marked the end of military rule, that the right to vote was extended to all adult Peruvians. Prior to that, those considered 'illiterate' (mainly those of indigenous descent living in rural areas) were excluded from the political process. These Peruvians make up most of the half of Peru's 27 million inhabitants who live beneath the United Nations' poverty threshold, on incomes of less than US$2 per day. They stand most in need of the state's protection and encouragement. Instead, however, they are still widely viewed as second-class citizens. As recently as 2002, a group of lawyers in the southern city of Arequipa argued vociferously with us that Peru could make no progress until the vote was taken back by 'people with an education' – meaning themselves and the other 'white' elites living mainly in the coastal cities.

But these elites have seen their hold on power weakened over the past two decades. In 1985, Alan García led APRA to power for the first time since its creation in 1924. Although far from revolutionary by this time, it did bring new players into power, with a different approach to both national and international issues. This brought a determined reaction from the traditional sectors of society, but the next elections, in 1990, brought even more of an outsider to the presidency: the controversial figure of Alberto Fujimori.

Once in office, Fujimori and his unofficial intelligence service head, Vladimiro Montesinos, deliberately set out to further undermine democratic rule. They not only changed the national Constitution, but used every means from legislation to massive bribery to concentrate more power directly into their own hands. At the same time, Fujimori's ideas on 'modernising Peru' meant the wholesale acceptance of the neo-liberal privatisation programme, with the same negative effects that have been seen throughout Latin America: the destruction of full-time 'structured' employment in the name of 'labour flexibility', the further reduction of the role of the state in economic management, and, despite claims that privatisation would mean an end to state corruption, the opportunity for unscrupulous leaders to loot state coffers for private gain.

The level of corruption in Peru reached staggering proportions under Fujimori and Montesinos. The highest echelons of almost all the state institutions, from the armed forces to the judiciary, from politicians to media bosses, seemed anxious to get their hands on as much as they could as the Peruvian state was sold off. This was a new kind of dictatorship, unlike those suffered by so many Latin American countries in the 1970s and 1980s. Commentators spoke of a '*dictablanda*' rather than a '*dictadura*'. Although torture and terror tactics were used against the civilian population in the fight against rebel groups, the Fujimori regime was more concerned to subvert the entire state system in order to perpetuate itself in power.

It was when these attempts became blatant in the run-up to the 2000 elections – when Fujimori stood for a third time – that opposition to his regime began to grow. The people who demonstrated against him, or worked to make sure that the elections could be as free and fair as possible, came from many backgrounds. There were groups that had sprung up, often encouraged by grassroots church organisations, to protest against the violence that had claimed so many lives. There were other grassroots groups who resisted the government's take-over of their local initiatives, and trade unionists critical of the government's attacks on their rights. Also involved were regional movements who organised to fight against the Fujimori regime's increasingly centralising tendencies. And the human rights groups that had grown in reponse to the years of violence or to the autocratic government's increasing restrictions of civil liberties were also at the forefront of efforts to get rid of Fujimori and his 'Siamese twin' Montesinos.

When the Fujimori regime collapsed in a dramatic fashion and the 'Vladivideos' became public – Montesinos had video-taped the striking of many corrupt deals (see p. 53) – few Peruvians were prepared for the revelations of just how deep-seated the corruption had been throughout their society. Opposition to Fujimori gave way to often agonised debate among politicians, human rights advocates, and many other sectors, as to how Peru had come to be what one prominent psychoanalyst termed 'spiritually bankrupt'. This despair soon gave way, however, to a sense that the catastrophe had been so great that it actually provided an opportunity: the Peruvian state must be 'refounded'. The hope was that the effective and all-inclusive democracy that had apparently eluded political parties and everyone else throughout much of the past 50 years could finally be achieved, thanks to the widespread consensus and sense of common purpose generated by the struggle to topple Fujimori, and then deal with the consequences of what was revealed.

For eight months in 2000–2001, the transitional govern-ment under the veteran politician Valentín Paniagua made strenuous efforts to begin reforms in many areas. Dozens of top officials and armed forces' officers who were shown to have been closely involved in Montesinos' corruption were put in jail. New heads of the judiciary, the police and the armed forces were brought in, with a mission to overhaul these areas and make them more transparent and responsive to ordinary Peruvians' needs. A Truth and Reconciliation Commission was set up to investigate the political violence that had affected so many Peruvians between 1980 and 2000. Efforts were made to begin a new political dialogue that would strengthen representative democracy and prevent anything like the Fujimori regime ever happening again.

These efforts were at first continued by President Alejandro Toledo, who won office in 2001 thanks chiefly to his credentials as an opponent of Fujimori. He was careful to incorporate a wide variety of political currents into his Cabinet, and to support the debates on how to reform the state and political life. Soon, however, faced with increasing unpopularity and unrest on the streets, President Toledo appeared to retreat, and increasingly relied on friends and cronies to administer what were often confused and unconvincing policies. It was not long before there were accusations of corruption against him and his supporters, and his popularity rating fell into single figures. The National Accord with which his term in office began soon splintered.

There were some notable achievements during Toledo's term in office. At the end of August 2003 the Truth and Reconciliation Commission produced its report, detailing the extent of the political violence which it calculated had led to nearly 70,000 deaths. The new law on political parties, passed in September 2003, sought to strengthen Congress against the executive, and to promote the creation of strong political groupings that would be more transparent and democratic in their own internal workings. In the same year, in an attempt to decentralise political power and influence, the first elections for regional parliaments took place, creating, in theory at least, more responsible devolved government with budgets to be spent at the local level.

Yet despite these successes, any sense of 'refounding' Peruvian democracy proved elusive. President Toledo himself appeared more concerned with survival, especially after what happened to the short-lived presidencies in neighbouring Ecuador and Bolivia, than to press ahead with a truly reforming agenda. Many of those who had agreed to participate in his government's attempts at reform, such as Susana Villarán, one of the authors of this book (appointed ombudswoman for the police), soon became disillusioned about the possibilities for real change, and left office. Fernando Rospigliosi, a lawyer who had been prominent in the struggle to prevent Fujimori winning a third term in office, was interior minister three times under President Toledo, leaving on each occasion because he felt that he did not have the president's backing.

At the same time, the economic legacy left by the Fujimori regime, with its privatisation and encouragement of foreign investment, has caused repeated popular protests. As in other Andean countries, there was dismay at the multinational take-over of public utilities such as water and electricity. In June 2002, this led to violent protests in the southern city of Arequipa and the declaration of a state of emergency. Similar concerns have been expressed about the impact of mining. This is a booming sector in the Peruvian economy, with fresh foreign investment having helped to double export earnings in recent years. But the transnational firms who have moved in have a chequered record when it comes to the environmental and social impact of their activities, while local analysts have expressed concerns that, as so often in the past, Peru's riches are being stripped out without bringing lasting benefits in terms of employment or helping to develop other areas of the economy.

The aim of this book is twofold. First, to look at how badly trust in representative democracy in Peru was undermined in the 1990s, and in particular at how Alberto Fujimori's authoritarian regime was able to pervert many of the state institutions for his own ends. Secondly, to consider what the president and government elected in 2006 need to do to pick up the pieces and help Peru to cement true democratic rule. If this proves impossible, Peru seems fated to endure yet more autocratic governments, with leaders chosen for their charisma, their promises, their TV style, but representing little beyond their own interests and those of the clique around them.

Picking up the pieces in Peru means taking effective measures to end social exclusion, allowing everyone – from the poor Aymara- and Quechua-speaking peasants to the tribes of Amazonia and the black Peruvians of the Pacific coast, to women who are still often only afforded a secondary role – to have a proper voice in the country's future. It means continuing the reforms of state institutions that were begun with high hopes following the ousting of Fujimori and Montesinos, and strengthening the many efforts to get rid of corruption in public life. It means restoring a sense of democratic dignity to a country that has, particularly in the years of the Fujimori regime, been ruled by people who have seen their positions of power as an opportunity to plunder the state, to undermine and manipulate institutions on their own behalf, and, in so doing, to destroy the belief of Peruvians that the state represents them and seeks their best interests.

Nick Caistor and Susana Villarán
Lima, 2006

1
The Tsunami

... *y total corrupción hay en todos lados*
que por cinco lucas me compro un diputado
un juez, un fiscal, un par de abogados
un arquitecto o en su defecto
un novelista, un par de periodistas,
un arzobispo, un cardenal
una virgen que llora o una virgen de verdad
y quizá hasta Fujimori ...

So what, there's corruption everywhere
For five bucks I can buy a congressman
a judge, a prosecutor, a couple of lawyers
an architect, or failing that
a novelist and a pair of journalists
an archbishop, a cardinal
a crying virgin or even a real one
perhaps even Fujimori himself...

Nosequien y los Nosecuantos[1]

The image that ushered Alberto Fujimori on to the political scene in 1989 could not have been more different from the ones that brought about his downfall a decade later. The earlier one showed the young presidential candidate astride a tractor, wearing his trademark simple white shirt, dark trousers and white socks, waving cheerily to largely imaginary supporters. The message accompanying the image, 'Honesty – Technology – Work', was guaranteed to appeal to all those Peruvians fed up with politicians making extravagant promises about bringing progress to Peru, only to leave them empty-handed yet again.

In the early days of the presidential campaign, the Peruvian electorate knew little of this surprise candidate. At the time, he was the rector of an agricultural university (at La Molina, on Lima's southern outskirts). His reputation as an efficient administrator was limited to academic circles, although he had come to the attention of the then president, Alan García, who had helped him to secure a position as presenter of a weekly early morning television programme on farming matters on the state-run Channel 7, the channel most watched in the Peruvian interior.

Alberto Fujimori was born in Lima, Peru on 28 July 1938 (see Box) to Japanese immigrant parents. His father eventually owned a small tyre-repair business in Lima, and the young Alberto spoke Japanese at home and among the small community of Japanese-Peruvians who were to be so important in his subsequent political career. As with many first-generation immigrant families the world over, education was seen by the Fujimoris as a way to get ahead. Alberto opted for mathematics and agriculture, writing his thesis on the sweet potato, before becoming an academic. He gradually worked his way up in academic administration, but was never thought to be harbouring political ambitions beyond that sphere. As it turned out, his entry into the world of party politics at the end of the 1980s was ideally suited to him.

The 1989–90 presidential elections came at the end of what most Peruvians saw as a disastrous five years under the presidency of Alan García and the APRA movement. This was

---

Fujimori Nippon?

Officially, Alberto Fujimori was born in the Peruvian capital in 1938, four years after his parents immigrated to the country from Japan. In 1997, an investigation by *Caretas* magazine concluded that his birth certificate, from Miraflores in Lima, had been tampered with. The magazine suggested that he had in fact been born in Japan in 1934. If this were true, Fujimori would have been ineligible to be president, as only people born in Peru can hold that office.

In a further twist to the story, the magazine also said that Vladimiro Montesinos knew of Fujimori's true birthplace, but was using the knowledge as another means of blackmailing the president to grant him even wider powers in the intelligence services and the armed forces.

---

the first time that the once revolutionary APRA had been allowed to wield power (it had previously won elections, only to find its path to government blocked by the armed forces). At 35, García was the country's youngest ever president. But his populist economic policies divided Peru, especially after his 1987 move to nationalise the Peruvian banking system, while his refusal to comply with the level of payments of foreign debt called for by the IMF and other international lending agencies left the country isolated internationally.

The last years of his presidency saw runaway hyper-inflation, and a 25 per cent fall in per capita GDP between 1988 and 1990 put the economy back at levels not seen since the 1950s. The formal economy contracted to such an extent that, by the end of García's government, less than 10 per cent of the working population in Lima were estimated to have 'adequate' employment. More than half the inhabitants of the chaotically expanding capital were living in poverty.

As Carol Graham points out, perhaps even more detrimental during this period was the drastic reduction in state provision for such essential services as education, health and the police:

> At $12 per person per year, the Peruvian government spent 30 per cent less on health and education than it had in 1980. And while GDP fell by nine per cent from 1986 to 1990, social expenditure fell by 22 per cent. The access of the average Peruvian citizen to police protection and the judicial services, meanwhile, was virtually non-existent by the late 1980s.[2]

This sense of abandonment by the state was compounded by a much more direct and violent threat to ordinary life. This widespread violence was created by the struggle between the security forces and revolutionary groups, such as the Communist Party of Peru–*Sendero Luminoso* (Shining Path, which took its name from the early 20th century Peruvian political philospher Mariátegui), and the *Movimiento Revolucionario Tupac Amaru* (MRTA). *Sendero Luminoso* combined elements of nationalism with a Maoist belief in the violent take-over of state power and the need for permanent revolution. Led by a former university lecturer, Abimael Guzmán (also known as 'President Gonzalo') *Sendero* declared war on the Peruvian state in 1980, when it began a campaign of terror in the province of Ayacucho and other areas in the Andean highlands.

The *Senderistas* claimed that only through revolution could the campesinos escape poverty and domination by a political class that had never had their interests at heart. Paradoxically, their arguments won converts in the interior provinces among the more educated lower middle classes, while the poorest peasants remained suspicious of the revolutionaries.

The armed forces became directly involved in counterinsurgency operations in Ayacucho in 1983–84. By declaring a state of emergency in many provinces of Peru, President García allowed the armed forces to extend their control until half the population was ruled by military rather than civilian authorities. Millions of poor Peruvians found themselves caught between state violence and the unwelcome coercion of rebel groups supposedly fighting on their behalf. This situation only served to underline the distance of the indigenous highland groups from the Peruvian state, as well as from politicians of all persuasions.

President García's failure to control this spiralling violence, in addition to the economic chaos his populist policies had created, meant that by the end of his term in office he and his APRA party were massively unpopular. Worse still for democratic rule in Peru, there was a general feeling of apathy mixed with widespread cynicism towards all politicians. Civilian rule had been re-established for only a little more than a decade, but it was already regarded as being unable to keep its promises.

This disaffection showed itself clearly in the 1989–90 election campaign. The front-runner at the beginning of the campaign was a political outsider, the novelist Mario Vargas Llosa. His books had explored Peruvian society, from the early anti-military novel *The Time of the Hero* and the political debate of *Conversation in the Cathedral,* to *The Storyteller* and other books of the 1980s. Like many young Latin American intellectuals of the 1960s, Vargas Llosa had begun as a committed left-winger in literature as well as in his political beliefs. But his feeling, shared by other writers, that Castro's rule in Cuba had created an oppressive regime rather than a Latin American version of egalitarian socialism, led him to a thorough-going political re-appraisal. As he grew older, he came increasingly to equate the freedom of individual expression with the freedom of choice espoused by 'free-marketeers' such as the economist

Friedrich Hayek or prime minister Margaret Thatcher in Britain.

What brought Vargas Llosa directly into Peruvian politics was his dismay at Alan García's take-over of the banking system. As he tells it in his autobiographical memoir, *A Fish in the Water*, he was jogging along the beach with his wife Patricia at the northern resort of Punta Sal when he heard the news: 'Once more in its history Peru has taken yet another step backward toward barbarism,' he told her, concluding: 'The nationalizations that had been announced would bring more poverty, discouragement, parasitism, and bribery to Peruvian life. And furthermore, in either the long run or the short, they would fatally damage the democratic system that Peru had recovered in 1980, after 12 years of military rule.'[3]

Vargas Llosa soon put himself at the head of a movement called *Libertad* (Freedom) to fight García, out of which emerged the *Frente Democrático* (FREDEMO) movement to fight the elections. The Front's platform was based on Vargas Llosa's political and philosophical beliefs – pushing back the state in favour of individual effort and choice, and allowing market forces and competition to counteract bureaucracy and corruption. Vargas Llosa undoubtedly saw himself as the Enlightenment candidate, bringing the light of reason to 'backward' Peru, and thought he could repeat the 'liberal' victories of Fernando Collor de Mello in Brazil, and Violeta Chamorro, who had driven out the Sandinistas after ten years of revolution in Nicaragua.

In order to try to secure a nationwide presence for the elections, Vargas Llosa allied himself with *Acción Popular*, the traditional opponents of APRA, and the smaller *Partido Popular Cristiano* (PPC). This gave many voters the impression that, instead of offering a clean break with the past, FREDEMO was simply the old, discredited political parties in a fresh guise, and this eventually proved to be one of the main reasons for its failure. In the run-up to the first round of voting, however, Vargas Llosa's smoothly-run campaign seemed to sweep everything before it.

Alberto Fujimori himself entered the fray late. At first he made an impression only in the poorer areas around the capital, and had little or no national impact. For many weeks he was not given a chance. He had few campaign funds: many of his materials were home-made by his eager family. He had no political record, and indeed was largely unknown outside university circles, apart from his TV programme. But he did have several advantages, which turned out to be crucial.

Somewhat surprisingly, one of the main ones was sustained support from the incumbent president, Alan García. As his term in office was drawing to its chaotic close, García realised that the APRA candidate, Luis Alva Castro, was on to a hiding to nothing, and was determined at all costs to prevent Vargas Llosa gaining power. He therefore lent Fujimori the backing of the state in various important areas. Interestingly, given how important it was shortly to become under Vladimiro Montesinos, García supplied Fujimori with intelligence information gathered by the National Intelligence Services (SIN). This included phone tapping of the other candidates' campaign strategies in order to keep Fujimori informed of their tactics. García's own view of the man almost everyone now knew as 'El Chino' is recorded by Sally Bowen: 'He's providential but he's dangerous. He is silent, introverted, calculating. It's difficult to know if he is just orientally inscrutable or a very clever politician. He could be extremely good,' García told reporters shortly before the election.[4]

Fujimori also won the backing of small business organisations, where the 45,000-strong Japanese-Peruvian community had considerable influence. As his first vice-presidential running mate he chose the head of the small and medium-sized manufacturers' association, Maximo San Román, like himself an 'outsider' because he came from the Quechua-speaking heartland of Cuzco and was of indigenous stock. Fujimori also secured the backing of the evangelical Christians, whose numbers had increased substantially over the previous two decades, particularly among the lower middle classes, as they became disillusioned with what the hierarchical Roman Catholic church had to offer them.

Most importantly, what became known as the 'Fujimori tsunami' or tidal wave drew its backing from all those Peruvians who considered that they had never been represented by the 'white' coastal elite of cities like Lima, Arequipa, or Trujillo. These were the majority of Peruvians who lived as impoverished peasants in the Andean highlands or the eastern jungle areas, and those who had moved to the cities in search of work and better prospects, only to find themselves living in even worse poverty in the *pueblos jóvenes* or shanty towns.

In some of the highland regions, it was only in the 1960s that the serfdom inherited from the Spanish colonial system had finally been abolished, and it was not until the return of civilian rule in 1980 that some two million Peruvians who could not read or write were finally given the identity papers that proved them to be fully-fledged citizens. They were also the ones who suffered most in the violent struggle between revolutionary groups and the armed forces.

These people saw Alberto Fujimori as someone much closer to themselves than Vargas Llosa. Like them, he was small and dark-skinned; like many of these Quechua speakers, he spoke Spanish as a second language, using simple phrases, not the suspiciously elegant constructions of his rival. As an agricultural engineer, he could talk of their daily problems on the land and of making ends meet rather than in the theoretical terms employed by the front-runner.

As a result of this growing identification with 'el Chino', Fujimori rose rapidly in the opinion polls. A fortnight before the first round of voting in April 1990, even Vargas Llosa had to concede that he was facing a serious challenge. In the first round, Vargas Llosa won 27.6 per cent to Fujimori's 24.5 per cent, but despite coming first, the novelist knew that APRA and the left-wing voters would not support him in the second round. And so it proved. In the run-off ballot, the little-known man on the tractor gained 56 per cent of the vote, to become the third president to take office since the restoration of democratic rule in 1980.

> I voted for 'El chino' because I'd seen him on the TV. He was on an early morning programme every week, sitting on his tractor and talking about problems in the countryside. He seemed to know much more about life up here in the highlands than any of the other candidates. And he didn't wear a suit, he dressed just like us.
> Mario from Sicuani on why he voted for Alberto Fujimori in 1990

It was one thing to win the elections, quite another to govern. During the weeks of campaigning, Fujimori had improvised ideas and plans, but appeared to have no well-defined political programme. According to a close early collaborator, Hernando de Soto (author of the influential book El Otro Sendero [The Other Path], which praised Peru's informal economy for its resilience and adaptability, suggesting that it might provide a solution to Peru's chronic economic problems), this was in part due to Fujimori's character: 'He's a political realist. He isn't against ideology but he just doesn't think that way: he is essentially a pragmatist. He reached out for formulas to confront the economic situation: he used intuition and he used facts.' But intuition and a quick grasp of the facts are not enough to provide a solid platform for government, and the newly elected president had to cast around quickly for support.

The elected members of Cambio 90, the political movement formed in the wake of his victory, reflected the heterogeneous origins of his electoral victory: seven of the new senators were evangelists; three were university professors; two were lawyers specialising in land disputes. From the start, it seemed clear that the new president had little interest in Cambio 90 except as congressional cannon-fodder: the grouping never even held a party convention, and at no point was it used as a forum for ideas or policy creation. The deputies themselves showed little political initiative, and never elaborated any coherent policies.

Cambio 90 did not guarantee Fujimori a majority in Congress, but the FREDEMO opposition was split after Vargas Llosa quit politics in disgust at losing the election, while APRA was still suffering from the negative effects of five years in office; the result was that between them they could not mount a serious challenge to the government. In addition, some three quarters of the new Congress were political newcomers, and their lack of political experience was largely responsible for Fujimori being given Congressional authority on no less than 15 occasions to rule by decree. Fujimori used this freedom to bring in new laws covering everything from the penal code, to reforms of the judicial, tax and banking systems.

Instead of turning to Cambio 90, Fujimori chose from the start to govern with a group of close advisers. Most prominent among these were his own family: his wife Susana, his younger brother Pedro, and in particular his elder brother Santiago. Santiago has been called the 'palace shadow', and it was he who suggested many of the key ministerial and civil service appointments, as well as deciding on where Fujimori should travel abroad.

Outside the family, Fujimori relied on key allies, who

defined the Fujimori regime and eventually led to its downfall. By far the most important of these was the man Peruvians came to dub the president's 'Siamese twin': Vladimiro Lenin Montesinos Torres.

Vladimiro Montesinos was from a traditional family in the southern city of Arequipa. As a young man, he chose to enter the army, and during the period of military rule from 1968 to 1980 soon rose to the rank of Captain. In 1973 he became a special adviser to the prime minister, General Edgardo Mercado Jarrín, supplying him with intelligence information. At the same time, he apparently began to pass information to the US embassy about Peru's arms purchases from the Soviet Union.

As a reward, he was invited to the United States, which he visited in 1976. His host there wrote in his report on Montesinos' trip to Washington: 'He is a firm friend of the United States, and the results of his visit will accrue benefits for both nations for many years to come.'[5] Unfortunately for Montesinos, he had left Peru using fake travel documents, and was spotted in Washington by suspicious Peruvian army superiors. On his return to Peru, his house was searched, and he was cashiered and jailed for forging documents and selling state secrets to a foreign power. It was while in jail that he began to retrain as a lawyer.

He soon put this training to good use. Freed from jail after only a year because he was suffering from hepatitis, he began, as a lawyer, to look for clients. During the 1980s, he became known as the defender of Colombian drugs traffickers wanted in Peru. The journalist Gustavo Gorriti puts it this way: 'He was the lawyer to the narcos but also so much more. He offered a complete service. He was connected to the court secretary; he had corrupt judges, corrupt prosecutors, police. And he was good: quick on his feet, a workaholic, audacious, unscrupulous.'[6]

In 1990 an old friend, Francisco Loayza, put Montesinos in touch with the president-to-be. At the time, accusations were surfacing that Fujimori had not paid tax on several real estate transactions. Montesinos soon sorted the problem out, getting the courts to shelve the case until after the elections. Once Fujimori had won, of course, he was safe: there was no question of the head of state being brought before the courts. Montesinos was quick to convince the president that he could provide essential links not only to the Peruvian armed forces but also to the CIA and other US agencies. Although never officially appointed, Montesinos became the linkman between the president and Peru's National Intelligence Service (SIN), which quickly gave him immense power. The new president soon came to trust Montesinos even more than his own family, and certainly more than his prime minister or anyone in the Cambio 90 movement.

To survive in power in the early days of his presidency, Fujimori also needed to keep the armed forces on his side. They had relinquished power in 1980, but by the end of the García government there was considerable military unrest, particularly among middle-ranking officers. These officers felt that the civilian government did not adequately understand the threat posed by the insurgent groups, and were frustrated that there was not firmer support for their struggle. They got as far as elaborating the *Plan Verde* (Green Plan), which outlined Peru's need for a joint civilian–military government with shared objectives for at least 20 years, in order to rid the country of 'subversives' and to put it back on track economically.

Almost immediately after the election, Montesinos and the SIN convinced Fujimori that there was a military plot to overthrow him. They persuaded him to seek refuge in the *Círculo Militar* (the military club in the Jesús María district of Lima). It was apparently during this time that the discontented officers discussed their 'Green Plan' with him and enlisted his support.

By this time, the armed forces' economic ideas were very different from those espoused by the Velasco government in the late 1960s. The *Plan Verde* called for large-scale privatisations, and a sharp reduction in the role of the state in the economy. What they were proposing was a Peruvian version of the free-market policies they saw as having been so successful under General Pinochet in neighbouring Chile.

Whether or not Fujimori actually agreed to implement the military's plan, privatisation and a drastic reduction of the role of the state in the economy were the chief elements in his shock economic programme (the 'Fujishock', put forward in August 1990, when inflation hit 400 per cent). Fujimori announced three basic aims: to bring hyperinflation under control, to sell off loss-making state concerns and bolster tax revenues in order to reduce the government deficit, and to return Peru to the international lending community in order to finance fresh projects. Fujimori and his economics minister Hurtado Miller did not hesitate to speak of the 'moralising' effect of these measures, which they claimed would put a stop to the corruption and waste typical of state enterprises, as well as bringing the healthy benefits of free competition to bear on the unfairly protected sectors of national industry.

In the short term, this led to a massive hike in prices for fuel, transport and other services, which had previously been controlled, and pushed unemployment still higher. By the end of 1991, more than two thirds of Peruvians were estimated to be living in poverty, half of whom were classified as suffering extreme poverty, unable to purchase even the minimum food basket. In 1991, an outbreak of cholera, a disease not seen in Latin America since the 19th century, marked its re-appearance in Peru. More than 1,000 people died, and a further 150,000 were affected.

By 1993, however, strong growth had returned to the Peruvian economy, and inflation had been brought down to a manageable 15 per cent. Foreign capital began to flow back to Peru, as investors snapped up the privatised companies, especially in the mining sector. What few people realised at the time was how these measures to enforce orthodox neo-liberal economic policies were being used for personal profit by Fujimori, Montesinos and high-ranking members of the armed forces and other sectors.

In order to push through these measures, Fujimori was determined not to be fettered by the traditional political parties in Congress, which he called the 'coimacracia' (bribocracy). Most of his economic policies were brought in by decree, and his authoritarian style was plain in other areas of government.

Chief among these was the fight against the violent revolutionary groups. At the end of the 1980s, Shining Path had extended its operations out of the remote highlands and brought terror to the streets of Peru's cities. Bombs were a daily occurrence, and there was a general sense of fear and unease. 'President Gonzalo' boasted that there was a 'strategic equilibrium' between the rebel forces and the state, and that the revolutionaries would eventually triumph because of their greater commitment and determination.

It was over the means to be adopted to combat these rebel groups that Fujimori ran into most resistance in Congress. Many of the opposition members insisted that it was a political battle as much as a military one. At the end of 1991, Congress even rejected his proposals for amplifying the role of the armed forces, a reaction Fujimori described at the time as 'irresponsible, sterile, anti-historical, and anti-national.'

Despite this opposition, Fujimori decreed that the president was to have the power to appoint the heads of all the branches of the armed forces, and that promotion should not be by seniority. Soon afterwards he placed his second key ally, General Nicolas de Bari Hermoza Rios, in the post of head of the joint chiefs of staff, and renewed him in that position year after year. As Sally Bowen remarks, Hermoza was so useful 'because he was a general without prestige, not exactly brilliant but manipulable'.[7]

But Fujimori went further than that in his efforts to rule without any checks or balances. Late in the evening of Sunday 5 April 1992, tanks emerged on to the streets of Lima and other cities. This was what became known as the '*autogolpe*' or 'palace coup'. Congress was closed down, the Supreme Court suspended, and opposition politicians and journalists rounded up. Fujimori declared a state of emergency, and prepared to rule by decree at the head of what he called a Government of Emergency and National Reconstruction. A majority of Peruvians, especially in the poorer sectors, applauded the move. Fujimori himself told the Brazilian magazine *Veja*:

> I think that in Latin America in general, democratic institutions are not prepared to bring in change. The fundamental difference in Peru is that someone appeared who could lead the people forward. That someone was the President of the Republic. I was the protagonist who brought what was bound to happen to a head. If I hadn't, the explosion would have occurred in the streets.[8]

The international community was not so impressed. The OAS and the United States sharply criticised the move. The Bush (senior) administration announced that it would halt all non-humanitarian aid to Peru, and spoke of imposing economic sanctions. The outrage was short-lived, however, as it became clear that there was no alternative to Fujimori. A few weeks later, US Under-Secretary of State Bernard

Massacres at La Cantuta and Barrios Altos

Both these massacres are thought to have been carried out by an army death squad commanded by a Major Santiago Martín Rivas. It operated under orders from army commander General Hermoza and Montesinos, and was known as the Grupo Colina.

The Barrios Altos massacre took place on 3 November 1991. A group of six hooded men burst into a barbecue being held by a group of ice-cream sellers in the run-down slum area of Barrios Altos in Lima. Fifteen people, including an eight-year-old boy, were killed in bursts of machine-gun fire. Press reports concluded that the death squad was the Grupo Colina. The massacre was a reprisal for a *Sendero Luminoso* attack on a presidential guard vehicle in which several soldiers died. According to intelligence apparently received by Montesinos, members of *Sendero* were posing as ice-cream sellers, and as a result he ordered the killings.

A judicial investigation in 1995 identified five of the six soldiers responsible for the massacre. The criminal investigation against them proceeded in the Supreme Court for Military Justice. The prosecution and punishment of the five individuals was blocked by Amnesty Law No. 26479 on 14 June 1995. Two days later, after a judge on the Sixteenth Criminal Court of Lima declared that the amnesty law violated constitutional guarantees and international obligations under the American Convention on Human Rights, Congress passed Amnesty Law No. 26492, which broadened the scope of the previous amnesty law. This prevented the criminal prosecution and punishment of those responsible for the Barrios Altos massacre.

The La Cantuta killings caused an even greater stir. On 18 July 1992, a death squad snatched a lecturer and nine students from the La Cantuta university campus east of Lima. The kidnapped were never again seen alive. Several months later, apparently following a tip-off by a group of more 'constitutionalist' army officers, the whereabouts of the victims was made public, and Hermoza and Montesinos were implicated.

In July 1993, journalists and forensic specialists found the burnt remains of the La Cantuta victims. There followed a protracted legal battle against 25 members of the armed forces, including Hermoza and Montesinos. The Supreme Court – handpicked by Fujimori – ruled that the case should be heard by a military court. Eventually, 11 of those named were found guilty, and sentenced to between 2 and 20 years. Thanks to the 1995 Amnesty Law, all were set free.

Since the fall of the Fujimori–Montesinos regime, strenuous efforts have been made to link them both to these killings. This is especially important in the case of Fujimori, as crimes against humanity of this sort are grounds for deportation even from Japan.

Aronson declared that it was for the Peruvians to decide their own political future, stressing: 'neither we nor the OAS are seeking a return to the *status quo ante*. Peru is a country in deep crisis which needs a deep reform.'

By now firmly convinced of his position as the arbiter of the national will, over the following months in 1992 Fujimori decreed a series of anti-terrorism laws, which severely limited many basic freedoms. The right to *habeas corpus* and the right of assembly were restricted; security forces could enter and search premises without a warrant, and could hold people suspected of terrorism for 30 days without charge. Many individuals found themselves facing military rather than civilian courts. When they were tried in court it was often by 'faceless' judges, whose identity was concealed in order to protect them from terrorist attack.

Even more damaging was Decree Law 25475, known as

the *Ley de Arrepentimiento* (Repentance Law). This decree encouraged rebel fighters or supporters to turn themselves in and face shorter prison sentences in return for information on others. This led to several thousand innocent people being accused and subsequently jailed, often merely on hearsay. Others were tried, convicted and sentenced *in absentia*. In June 1992, Decree Law 25564 lowered the age of criminal responsibility from 18 to 15.

Human rights groups inside Peru and abroad protested at the harshness of these measures, but President Fujimori himself put a very different slant on them, declaring in July 1993: 'This government in particular has a policy that clearly defends human rights. There is no other way to explain that today our jails are filled to the brim with terrorists.'[9]

But it was thanks more to good old-fashioned detective work rather than any of these draconian decrees that brought Fujimori his greatest success in the fight against the rebel groups. On 12 September 1992, Abimael Guzmán was captured without a fight in the flat where he lived in hiding above a dance school in a middle-class Lima neighbourhood. Although *Sendero* committed several more atrocities in the following months, the capture of Guzmán and several other leaders proved to be the turning point in the battle against the subversives. President Fujimori was quick to claim the responsibility for this victory, which again increased his popularity.

Although Fujimori steadfastly rejected international criticism over human rights in Peru, he did listen to the Organisation of American States when they took him to task for continuing to rule without any permitted political activity, in Congress, at regional and municipal level, or on the streets. His response, prompted by Montesinos, was to annul the 1979 constitution and call a Constituent Assembly to draw up a new one. Thanks to the dramatic seizure of

The First Lady Regrets

At the start of his political career, Alberto Fujimori's wife, Susana Higuchi, was one of his closest allies. Twelve years younger than him, she had graduated as an engineer before branching out into construction and housing. She even made many of the first posters promoting her husband as the 'honest Chinaman'. As first lady, she devoted herself to 'good works' and charities.

This all changed in March 1992, when out of the blue she accused her husband's family of diverting clothing and funds donated by solidarity groups in Japan. After this, she made further extraordinary claims that she was being held prisoner in the presidential palace, and had even been tortured.

These protests led to an official separation, after which, in 1994, Higuchi launched her own political movement, *Armonía Siglo XXI* (21st Century Harmony). This was designed as a vehicle to support her attempt to stand as a candidate against her husband in the 1995 presidential elections. Fujimori quickly saw to it that the compliant Congress rushed through a law banning presidential relatives from standing for elections, in what became known as 'Susana's Law'.

After 22 years of marriage, the couple were divorced, and their daughter Keiko Sofia became the president's official companion. Higuchi again complained of ill-treatment by her former husband, and denounced him as increasingly authoritarian.

As protests against the president grew in the run-up to the 2000 re-election campaign, Susana returned to the political fray, this time as a congressional candidate for the *Frente Independiente Moralizador* (FIM). On her campaign trail she wielded a broom to show that she wanted to sweep the presidential palace clean, and denounced her husband's acts of corruption. She was elected to Congress in 2001, but resigned her seat a year later. One of her most recent accusations was that in July 1990, just before becoming president for the first time, her former husband had received a donation of US$12 million to be used for poor children in Peru, which he deposited in a personal bank account in Tokyo.

Guzmán and signs that crippling hyperinflation had been brought under control, Fujimori and his supporters won a clear majority of the 80 seats in the assembly.

The main provisions of the new Constitution further strengthened Fujimori's position as head of state: Congress lost its second chamber, and more importantly, for the first time in modern Peruvian history, the possibility of re-election was created (though for one further term only). This obvious concentration of power in the hands of the executive was possibly a step too far: the regime only narrowly won the referendum held in September 1993 to approve the new constitution. This was the first time that President Fujimori had seen his support waver since coming to office.

What was not known in these first years of the Fujimori regime was the extent to which he and Montesinos were already involved in illicit dealings aimed at accruing millions of dollars for themselves. But an inkling of what was going on had surfaced as early as March 1992. On that occasion, none other than Fujimori's wife, Susana Higuchi, denounced her husband's relatives to the press for misusing money and clothes donated to Peru by various charities in Japan (see box above). According to Higuchi, Fujimori's sister and other women in the family even took the choicest pieces of clothing for themselves, and sold off other items through second-hand shops.

Far more lucrative and at the same time far more damaging to Peru's democracy was the involvement of leading figures in the government and armed forces in illegal drug smuggling. Throughout the 1980s, Peru had become one of the main suppliers of the coca paste that forms the basis of the cocaine smuggled to the United States and Europe after being processed in Colombia. The main coca-producing region in Peru is the Huallaga valleys in the remote north-east of the country.

The sums earned by the gangs arranging flights for shipping the coca paste to Colombia were enormous. These gangs are known to have bought off the local army and airforce commanders, and it was not long before Montesinos decided that he should be paid his share as well. Much of the evidence against him comes from one trafficker, Demetrio Chavez Peñaherrera, otherwise known as 'El Vaticano'. When placed on trial for illegal drug-running, El Vaticano gave convincing details of how he paid US$50,000 each month to Montesinos in order to avoid trouble with his flights across the border. El Vaticano also told the court that General Hermoza and the local commander received regular pay-offs.

At the same time, he claimed that he once 'asked Vladimiro Montesinos if President Fujimori knew about this. "Yes", he told me, "because without him you couldn't do a thing".'[10] Bowen and Holligan point out just what extraordinary power Montesinos wielded during those years:

> By the mid-1990s, Montesinos was in a highly unusual position: although never officially appointed, he was the Peruvian government's principal representative on counter-narcotics matters: he debated strategy with the CIA, the DEA and other US representatives. At the same time, he was also, by several accounts, the protector-in-chief of various mafias involved in the illegal drug trade in Peru.[11]

As we shall see in the next chapter, the money that Montesinos and, in all likelihood, President Fujimori himself made out of the illegal drugs trade was nothing compared to the huge amounts they siphoned off from the Peruvian state.

Notes

1. From a song by the Peruvian rock band Nosequien y los Nosecuantos.
2. Carol Graham and Stefano Pettinato, 'Assessing Hardship and Happiness: Mobility Trends and Expectations in the New Market Economies', Center on Social and Economic Dynamics Working Paper Series no. 7, Brookings Institution, Washington, DC, October 1999, p. 3.
3. Mario Vargas Llosa, *A Fish in the Water*, Faber & Faber, London, 1994, pp. 30, 31–32.
4. Sally Bowen, *The Fujimori File,* Peru Monitor, Lima, 2000, p. 20.
5. Thomas Catán, article in *Financial Times Magazine*, London 26 July 2003, p. 17.
6. Gustavo Gorriti, interview with authors, April 2004.
7. Bowen, op. cit., p. 67.
8. Quoted in Raúl E. Wiener, *El Reeleccionista*, Lima, 1998, p. 89.
9. Congreso de la República del Perú, *Informe final de la comisión especial de la investigación sobre los delitos cometidos entre 1990–2000*, Lima, 2002, p. 5.
10. Sally Bowen and Jane Holligan, *The Imperfect Spy: The Many Lives of Vladimiro Montesinos*, Peisa, Lima, 2003, p. 163.
11. Ibid., p. 167.

2
Privatisation and Corruption

During the decade that Alberto Fujimori was in power in Peru, some 220 state enterprises were sold off. These companies were often in key areas such as oil, electricity, communications, gas, mining, and agriculture and fisheries. The Peruvian state directly employed some 200,000 people, and public concerns accounted for 15 per cent of GDP, as well as 28 per cent of exports and 26 per cent of imports.

By adopting privatisation as one of his main economic goals, President Fujimori was following what had become orthodox thinking. The international political climate strongly encouraged privatisation. In the United States Ronald Reagan was stridently pro-business, while in Great Britain, Prime Minister Margaret Thatcher was using the windfall opportunity offered by the discovery and exploitation of North Sea oil to alter dramatically the composition of industry and open up new spaces for the private sector.

Alongside them, international institutions like the IMF and the World Bank were urging an end to the protectionist policies pursued by governments in the developing world as a way of helping national industry. The agencies argued that private investment was more dynamic, and that the state should take a back seat while competitive market forces helped to create a 'leaner', more efficient economy. What became known as the 'Washington consensus' was followed so eagerly by many Latin American governments that, as

Luigi Manzetti notes, 'between 1990–1996, Latin America and the Caribbean became the developing world's leaders in privatisation, accounting for 54% of the total proceeds ($82.4 billion).'[1]

One of the main arguments put forward by those pushing Peru and other developing countries into privatisation and other neo-liberal reforms – the reduction of the role of the state in the economy, the withdrawal of subsidies and protective tariffs for national economies – was that the competitive free market would substantially reduce economic and political corruption. This argument is briefly synthesised by Joseph S. Tulchin and Ralph H. Espach in their book *Combating Corruption in Latin America*:

> Since the end of the Cold War, as belief in the efficacy of democracy and free-market economies has spread around the world, a general consensus has developed that 1) in all systems, corruption has an overall negative effect on economic growth and stability and on democratic consolidation; and 2) the reduction of state bureaucracies and the encouragement of more transparent, free-market operations, along with improving the government's capacity to regulate these processes and then enforce the law, are the most effective methods of controlling corruption.[2]

Unfortunately, the optimistic assessment that privatisation would help to cut corruption in the region proved largely unfounded. In fact, the opposite seems to have happened. Time and again the benefits of privatisation were hijacked by those in power, and the billions of dollars generated did little to improve the lives of the majority of the people. In many cases, the new companies proved as inefficient as the old state-run ones, and the upsurge in unemployment that resulted from dismantling state concerns was not compensated for by the creation of new jobs in the private sector.

The flight of President Fujimori in November 2000 was the merely the most recent in a list of elected leaders forced to leave office. The list includes Fernando Collor de Mello in Brazil, Carlos Andres Pérez in Venezuela, and Fernando de la Rúa in Argentina. In addition, since stepping down, Presidents Carlos Salinas Gortari of Mexico, Carlos Menem of Argentina, Abdalá Bucarám of Ecuador and Miguel Alemán of Nicaragua, among others, have been accused of massive corruption.

Political corruption had always been a serious problem in many Latin countries, but as a Peruvian report after the fall of Fujimori and Montesinos argues, in the 1990s the problem changed in nature: 'corruption transferred from the area of administration to the very nucleus of political power. The [Peruvian] state became a servant of this corrupting nucleus, and co-opted, eliminated or neutralised all those who either inside the state apparatus or in civil society seemed to be hostile to this political project.'[3]

This new and pernicious form of corruption was evident in many other Latin American countries. In Brazil, for example, President Collor de Mello's career closely paralleled that of Fujimori. A political outsider, he created his own movement to back his candidacy in 1990. During the campaign, he offered no coherent political platform, but on the very day he took office he announced his *Plano Collor*, designed to bring hyperinflation and government spending under control thanks to a sweeping programme of privatisations. His closest adviser, P.C. Farias, was the mastermind behind the sell-offs, and also allegedly the one who diverted many of the funds raised into the pockets of the president and his closest allies. As with Fujimori, this massive corruption was accompanied by rhetoric from Collor de Mello lambasting the traditional political parties for all they had stolen from the state. He also took advantage of the widespread mistrust of politicians and the economic crisis to misappropriate huge sums of money.

The big difference between Collor's Brazil and Fujimori's Peru was the fact that, as early as 1992, a parliamentary investigation was begun into Collor's illicit dealings, and he resigned in order to escape impeachment at the end of that year.

In Argentina, President Menem pursued a similar political course. He too was an outsider, the governor of a small province who moved on to the national stage when he won the presidency at the end of 1989. The economic crisis at that time was so great that he was even sworn into office several months early, and he used the political disarray generated by this crisis to initiate a wide-ranging set of economic reforms. Like President Fujimori, he brought in privatisation by decree rather than through democratic debate; like his Peruvian counterpart, he redrew the Constitution to be able to continue in power. From early on in his first presidency, Menem and his closest associates were accused of manipulating the sell-off of state concerns for their own gain: the accusations ranged from taking bribes and kickbacks to being involved in money-laundering for drugs cartels. However, despite the fact that Menem faced as many as 20 financial scandals in his first term of office, and 20 ministers or advisers were forced to resign, in 1995 he was re-elected (as was Fujimori) with an increased majority.

Beyond the presidents, Vladimiro Montesinos may have been the greediest and most successful official to profit from the privatisations which took place throughout the subcontinent, but there were many others who plundered the state for personal gain. Perhaps Raúl Salinas de Gortari, the brother of the Mexican president who ruled from 1988 to 1994, comes closest to Montesinos in terms of sheer greed. On one occasion, he organised a dinner at which many of

Mexico's leading businessmen were encouraged to give donations of US$25 million each to the funds of the ruling Institutional Revolutionary Party (PRI) in return for 'special consideration' in the privatisation process. On another occasion, the new private owners of the former state telecommunications company allegedly paid him US$50 million to set up a 'venture capital fund' for future projects. From Argentina to Ecuador, from Panama to Paraguay, government officials took bribes and commissions from transfers of businesses out of the public sector.

Almost every stage of the process of selling state concerns to private bidders offered opportunities for corrupt dealing. At the outset, information on the companies involved could be sold to favoured buyers, or advisers who were hired to value a public firm could deliberately prefer one bidder. In Venezuela, for example, the First Bank of Boston was brought in to advise on the sale of the state airline, even though the Spanish company Iberia was a client of the bank – and Iberia were the eventual purchasers. In Argentina, there were huge scandals involving the US computer firm IBM. The US$585 million contract to supply the tax authorities with new computer systems was widely seen as exorbitant, especially as there was no proper public tendering process for the contract. Another US$250 million deal involving the Banco de la Nación also attracted a great deal of media attention, as it was plain that the contract was overpriced, and that many of those involved had taken bribes to push the deal through. IBM consistently maintained that they had done nothing illegal, but were just following the rules of the game.

On other occasions, state companies were sold in a manner that did not increase competition, but simply confirmed the successful private purchaser in a monopoly position in the national market. In several countries, including Peru, the lack of effective anti-trust legislation meant that these transfers were never challenged. The supposed benefits of greater competition and therefore lower prices to the consumer just did not come about. All too often, the sale simply transferred ownership to a much reduced number of individuals – often friends or political cronies of the president and his inner circle of advisers.

At the same time, the regulatory bodies, which should, according to the model, oversee the transfer of these companies and then supervise the new structures in a way beneficial to the consumers, have also been weak and deficient, or have been filled with the same old friends of the governing politicians and their friends. To add to all these factors, the lack of a truly independent judiciary in Peru, as elsewhere in Latin America, led to there being few lawsuits to keep the suspect practices in check at all.

The state sector sales under Fujimori and Montesinos in the 1990s are estimated to have raised more than US$9.2 billion for the government. But according to the special prosecutors investigating the extent of corruption during the Fujimori regime, only US$6.4 billion of this actually found its way into state coffers. Although exact figures are difficult to come by, it appears that more than US$2.8 billion was siphoned off either directly by Montesinos and Fujimori, or by all the other levels of officials involved in the deals. At the same time, according to Manuel Dammert, the proceeds that did reach the treasury from the selling-off of more than three-quarters of Peru's national industries were spent in three main areas: payment of the foreign debt, arms purchases for the military, and the 'president's perpetual re-election campaign'.[4] Almost all of this expenditure was designed to bolster the regime's position: the first by keeping the international community happy; the second by keeping the armed forces on side; the third to buy votes.

Montesinos, Fujimori and their cronies made money out

of privatisation in any number of ways. Commissions were charged to the private, usually foreign, companies bidding to take over the Peruvian concerns. A bonus was paid if the bid was successful. Assets were deliberately undervalued, and then part of the price of the concession was paid under the table to the ever-willing Montesinos (who busily videotaped the whole transaction). On other occasions, the state concerns were simply transferred to friends and associates of the two leaders. As early as 1993, it was Mario Vargas Llosa who argued in the Argentine newspaper *Clarín* that the privatisation process in Peru and elsewhere had gone badly awry:

> What principally happened with the privatisation efforts in Peru, Mexico, and Argentina does not differ much from the transfer of state monopolies into the hands of the large private entrepreneurs. This contradicts the moral reasoning behind privatisation: opening the markets and beginning the competition that will lead to the process of wealth creation.... Privatisation was used simply to inject fresh money into a bankrupt state through the corrupt sales of assets to the friends of the political leaders. Privatisation should be, on the contrary, the key element towards social and economic reform. It should allow people to participate in the system and give them economic independence.[5]

Neither Montesinos nor Fujimori seem to have been interested in using privatisation to spread the gospel of popular capitalism. Montesinos appears simply to have seen the state as a treasure chest to be plundered as he saw fit. Fujimori was more interested in the political gains to be had. First and foremost, the sell-offs offered a lifeline to the desperately under-financed state. In addition, by adopting the model strenuously promoted by the international community and the lending agencies, Peru was welcomed back into the global financial world. And in domestic politics, the privatisation of state concerns had the added benefit for Fujimori of weakening the position of the organised trade unions, many of which had been formed either by APRA or by militant left-wing groups. As in many other countries around the world, privatisation and 'labour flexibility' put the Peruvian trade unions on the defensive, and further fragmented opposition to the government.

Montesinos himself made money from the very start of the privatisation initiative. One of the first public auctions of a government-owned company was for the Banco del Comercio, and the lack of transparency surrounding this sale became typical. The CLAE group, which eventually bought the bank (where Montesinos had an interest), did not fulfil all the conditions stipulated under Peruvian banking laws, so the Banco de Comercio was declared exempt from those laws only a few hours before the auction. Nor did the agency in charge of privatisations, COPRI, demand any investment plan from the new purchasers, or any guarantees on employment or other essential points. As the president of COPRI said, 'we are going to sell, whatever the price'.

As well as using the privatisation process to make money, Montesinos (and, thanks to him, Fujimori) also milked the state in many other ways. The fate of the Military Pensions Fund provides a good example of Montesinos' way of working. The pension fund was set up under military rule in 1974 to look after members of the armed forces and their dependants – around 250,000 people. By 1992, the fund was estimated to be worth about US$90 million – until Montesinos moved in. He set himself up as head of the board overseeing the fund, and appointed friendly generals as the other board members. He also brought in three of his business associates, Alberto Venero, Luis Duturburu and Silvio Valencia Rosas, to administer the day-to-day running of the fund. He and his associates then proceeded to invest large amounts of it in their own interests. One purchase was of shares in Immobiliaria Las Americas, which owned the luxurious Hotel Las Americas in Miraflores, the smartest part of Lima, and other real estate.

According to the lawsuit brought against all those involved in running the Military Pensions Fund between 1992 and 2000, the fund in 1992 lent the then owners of the hotel (among whom was Silvio Valencia Rosas) a total of US$7 million. By 1993, when the original owners could not repay the loan, the fund managers decided to take 50 per cent of the shares in the loss-making company instead. They also paid the owners a further US$1.8 million for agreeing to the sale. In 1994, the owners offered to sell the remaining 50 per cent of the shares to the fund. The board commissioned a study to establish the going value of the hotel – and the firm which carried out the study was headed by none other than Alberto Venero. His company valued the hotel at US$27 million, which the fund managers accepted unanimously. (A later valuation by the National Valuation Council put the hotel's value in 1994 at some US$10.5 million).

Then in a further extraordinary move, the trustees of the Military Pensions Fund appointed the same company to run the hotel, including Montesinos' close associate Silvio Valencia Rosas. In this way, Montesinos transferred more than US$30 million from public funds to his private business dealings.

In this particular case, some idea of how Montesinos' network of illicit dealings all dovetailed together was revealed in further anti-corruption hearings in 2002. Former congressman Jorge Polack was accused by Montesinos' private secretary, Matilde Pinchi Pinchi, of having received almost US$500,000 to transfer his allegiance from the *Unidad Nacional* party to Fujimori after the disputed 2000 elections. Polack was also the owner of a radio station, Radio

Libertad, which broadcast to popular sectors in the Peruvian capital. In another 2002 hearing, it transpired that the radio had signed three advertising contracts worth some US$120,000 in August 2000, and had been paid for them in cash. The three advertising campaigns were for the Military Pensions Fund, the Banco de Comercio, and the Hoteles Las Americas chain. So Montesinos not only directly bribed politicians whose support he thought he could buy, he also ensured that these people were indebted to him for the success of their businesses.

The Military Pensions Fund is just one example of the hundreds of corrupt deals in which Vladimiro Montesinos was involved. President Fujimori continues to deny strenuously any involvement in the corruption practised by his unofficial adviser, but it seems impossible that he was unaware of the vast web of deceit being spun around him. Montesinos was quick to realise that the changes Fujimori was bringing to Peruvian society were so rapid and far-reaching that nobody could be certain what the rules of the game were any more, and he immediately took full advantage of this confusion for his own benefit. As Lawrence Whitehead remarks on high-level political corruption in Latin America, what is most frightening about the experience in Latin America in the 1990s is the way one kind of corruption almost inevitably led to another:

> The recently uncovered scandals in Brazil, Mexico, Argentina, and elsewhere indicate how easily one variety of high-level political corruption runs into another: how electoral corruption can lead to money laundering, complicity with *narcotraficantes* and eventually court rigging and even political assassination.[6]

At the time, little or nothing of the criminal activities going on behind the public facade of the Fujimori regime came to the surface in Peru. By 1993, the majority in Congress were

completely compliant, and as a result the legislature rarely
performed its function as a check on the executive. The
opposition political parties were in disarray. They were in the
galling position of still being regarded by a majority of
Peruvians as the corrupt ones – part of the old cliques which
Fujimori could blame for the disastrous situation in which
the country found itself. The trade unions were equally
unprepared for the assault on the state enterprises, and were
likewise accused of supporting the 'bad old ways'. They also
lost influence as the newly privatised firms laid off thousands
of workers, and banned union organisation.

Over the heads of Congress and the political classes,
Fujimori told Peruvians that the shock treatment he had
administered in economic, political and national security
areas was necessary because of the mess he had inherited.
And as his first term in office drew to a close in 1994–95, the
unlikely president could point to his government's significant
achievements. The violence that had torn Peru apart for more
than a decade had dwindled significantly. Poor peasants
returned to the central highlands and other areas worst
affected by the violence. The plague of hyperinflation had
also receded, and although there was little noticeable
improvement in terms of real employment, the government
message of new opportunities and choices still convinced
many. From 1993 on, economic growth returned to Peru,
reaching the previously unheard-of figure of 13 per cent in
1994, thanks largely to the sell-offs in the public sector and
the influx of foreign investment in mining, communications
and other sectors.

In order to convince Peruvians further that their future
well-being depended on its continuation in power, the
Fujimori government set out on a determined campaign to
co-opt or buy off independent initiatives that benefited the
poorest sectors. The well-established *Federación de Comedores*

Populares (Federation of People's Canteens) run by women in poor districts of Lima and elsewhere was undermined when the Fujimori government set up its own organisation for distributing food and offering it at subsidised canteens. In 1992, the National Food Aid Programme (PRONAA) was set up. Only those caterers who backed the government were included in this programme, and in the 1995 elections members were required to attend Fujimori's campaign meetings.

Social spending was co-ordinated through the Ministry of the Presidency. This became a key part of the government. A national plan for poverty reduction was drawn up, and hundreds of small projects identified – new schools, community kitchens, roads, electricity schemes and so on. In 1994, the IMF agreed that as much as US$876 million, which had been collected from privatisation, could be earmarked either for this programme or for infrastructure spending. The Fujimori government targeted projects that most interested them in terms of winning votes, often flying the candidate-president in by helicopter and making sure that the media covered the 'event'.

Fujimori's message at the 1995 opening of a new school in a poor district of Lima could not have been clearer:

> This is how I work, silently. You want a school for your children and here it is, for your sons and daughters to make use of. I don't make false promises. Be careful of those who come offering you things they don't deliver. You know who they are, and you also know that I carry out what I promise.[7]

In this way, poor Peruvians were made to understand that improvements to their situation depended directly on the president, and had nothing to do with the local authorities or any other political parties. And this combination of a direct, simple message with hidden coercion seemed to work.

A reporter stated that in some departments of Puno province in the south-east of Peru, 70 per cent of voters had been against Fujimori in the 1992 post-coup referendum, but, thanks mainly to direct government spending in the interim, 73–83 per cent supported him in the 1995 election.[8]

Just before the election, the Peruvian armed forces and Fujimori himself had an opportunity to redeem themselves on the military front. In January 1995, Peru suddenly found itself facing a foreign conflict. This was with its northern neighbour, Ecuador, in a border dispute that had rumbled on for more than a century. Ecuador had always claimed territory around the frontier in the Cordillera del Condor, seeing this as an access route to the Amazon, which would give Ecuadorean trade a way out to the Atlantic. The dispute had supposedly been settled by a conference in Rio de Janeiro in 1942, which established a border that both countries agreed to respect.

Occasionally however, the dispute flared up again, usually when Ecuador sent patrols into what Peru regarded as its sovereign territory. But in January 1995 Ecuadorean troops had set up several posts inside Peru, and refused to relinquish them. Its government claimed that this part of the border had not even been properly mapped in the 1940s, and that there was an 80-kilometre stretch that should by rights belong to them. At first, Peru was taken by surprise, and its poorly equipped army proved unable to dislodge the Ecuadoreans, who were backed by more capable planes and helicopters. Fujimori seized the opportunity to visit the front and show once again that he was personally in charge, and to reinforce his position as commander-in-chief. Determined to make political capital out of the incident, he first stated that Peru had recaptured the important post of Tiwinza (although later reports suggested that this was untrue), and that all Ecuadorean troops had been thrown out of Peruvian territory, and then declared a unilateral ceasefire. This high-risk strategy paid substantial dividends for the election campaign. Fujimori had defeated terrorism in Peru, he had conquered hyperinflation and got the economy growing again, and now he had not only defeated the old enemy, but had shown what a statesman he was by calling a truce.

Montesinos meanwhile was turning the conflict to advantage in his own way. Although the incursion by Ecuadorean forces could be said to have shown up the failings of his intelligence services, he was never criticised for it. But Peruvian intelligence did apparently get to hear of the deal the Ecuadoreans made to buy 8,000 FAL rifles and ammunition. The deal was brokered by a US-based arms supplier, Jean-Bernard Lasnaud. It also involved the Menem administration in Argentina, although that country was one of the guarantors of the 1942 treaty. According to Lasnaud several years later, Montesinos demanded US$2 million to keep quiet about having discovered the deal. The Ecuadorean authorities yielded to the blackmail, and are alleged to have paid the money into a Panamanian bank account.

By the end of this first term in office, therefore, the Fujimori–Montesinos–Hermoza triumvirate had clearly defined roles. Hermoza kept the armed forces happy. Fujimori was the public face of the regime, sold to the electorate as 'an ordinary Peruvian just like you'. But according to many observers, such as the French sociologist André-Marcel D'Ans, Montesinos' position at the centre of a spider's web, between armed forces, intelligence services and the presidential palace: 'made him the real head of state. Montesinos skilfully manipulated the isolation and political incoherence of a president whose obsession with power was quickly turning into an authoritarian delirium, and had no trouble turning the regime into a mafioso dictatorship.'⁹

Notes

1. Luigi Manzetti, *Privatization South American Style*, Oxford University Press, Oxford, 2000, p. 1.
2. Joseph S. Tulchin and Ralph H. Espach (eds), *Combating Corruption in Latin America*, Johns Hopkins University Press, Baltimore, 2000, p. 5.
3. Ministerio de Justicia del Perú, *Un Perú sin corrupción*, Lima, 2000, p. 3.
4. Manuel Dammert, *Fujimori–Montesinos, el estado mafioso*, Ediciones El Virrey, Lima, 2001, p. 118.
5. Mario Vargas Llosa, article in *Clarín*, Buenos Aires, 23 July 1993.
6. Lawrence Whitehead, 'High-level political corruption', in Tulchin and Espach, op. cit., p. 115.
7. Isabel Yépez del Castillo, in Claude Auroi and Sandra Bossio (eds), *A donde va el Perú?*, Institut Universitaire d'Etudes du Développement, Cuzco, 2002, p. 39.
8. C. Balbi, in ibid., p. 41.
9. André-Marcel D'Ans, in ibid., p. 26.

3

1995–2000
The Mafia State

For the first time in modern Peru, the new Constitution adopted by Fujimori and his political allies in 1993 allowed for the immediate re-election of the president. Many opposition figures claimed that because Fujimori had been in power before this new legislation was introduced, he was ineligible to stand again in the next election, due in April 1995. But in another demonstration of his contempt for the niceties of constitutional rule, Fujimori quickly announced he had every intention of standing. As before, he was backed by a loose alliance, now known as *Cambio-90 Nueva Mayoria*, which contained many first-time politicians and candidates who deserted other parties in the hope of profiting from his success.

Fujimori's main challenger was the veteran diplomat Javier Pérez de Cuellar, who was already 74 years old. Pérez de Cuellar's main successes had been won internationally as Secretary-General of the United Nations from 1982 to 1990. Pérez de Cuellar had spent most of his life working as a diplomat outside Peru, and hoped to present himself as someone untainted by the unseemly spectacle of the wrangling traditional political parties. 'I know how to negotiate and conciliate. I've spent my life doing it. I can assure governability in democracy.'[1]

In the event, President Fujimori won a second term in office at the first round of voting. He secured a large majority:

65 per cent to Pérez de Cuellar's 22 per cent. In his speech accepting Fujimori's victory, the defeated candidate sounded a prophetic warning: 'I recognize that the people have preferred to reward the defeat of terrorism and hyperinflation although they have not earned, at the same time, a democratic future with social development'.[2]

For his part, the newly re-elected 'honest Chinaman' was exultant:

> I hereby affirm that today political parties ended. The govern-
> ment works without political parties. It is a direct democracy
> where the executive is in contact with the people without the
> mediation of political organizations that here, like elsewhere,
> have failed. This is a model that has proven to be efficient in
> solving problems, a democratic model that I would not be sur-
> prised, modesty aside, if it were reproduced in other countries.[3]

So Alberto Fujimori emerged from the 1995 elections in a more secure position than ever before. His gamble of closing down the Congress in 1992 and pushing through a Constitution which reinforced the powers of the executive had paid off handsomely. He had won what were widely regarded as relatively free and fair elections against a distinguished opponent, and had the backing of two out of three Peruvians for further reforms. But any hope that this easy victory would lead him to open up the government or allow greater political debate and argument was quickly deflated. Even before he officially began his second term in office, Fujimori rushed two pieces of legislation through the still sitting Constituent Assembly, which clearly indicated the authoritarian nature of his rule.

The first of these, in May 1995, was a proposal that political parties would be required to collect signatures of support from at least 4 per cent of the voting population (almost half a million signatures) to be able to register for elections. In a country where political affiliation outside election periods is almost non-existent, this measure was clearly aimed at destroying the opposition parties.

A month later, this was followed up by even more controversial legislation. This was an amnesty law for all members of the police and armed forces accused of human rights violations from May 1980 onwards, and guaranteed exemption from any future charges. This move was designed to ensure the continuing support of the armed forces, who had long been concerned that they might some day be judged for their actions as their colleagues in Argentina had been. The amnesty meant that not only was the infamous Colina paramilitary group set free from prison, but that there could be no further investigations into abuses committed by the armed forces during the fight against the rebel groups, such as the controversial killings in Barrios Altos in Lima. When the judge investigating the killings, Antonia Saquicuray Sánchez, indicated that she was prepared to ignore the new law and continue with the case, the attorney-general, Blanca Nelida Colán Maguiño, ordered the closure of the investigation, and threatened the judge with dismissal.

The way in which this new amnesty law was passed was also typical of the Fujimori administration's way of staying just within the limits of legality, but of completely betraying the democratic spirit. The bill was brought to the Constituent Assembly for a vote without any warning late on the night of 14 June 1995, passed with no debate thanks to the government majority, immediately signed by President Fujimori, and by the next day had become law. In this way, any debate on the issue by the opposition or in the media was headed off.

Beyond this sleight of hand, from the start of Fujimori's second term in office he and Montesinos undertook an assault on Peru's democratic institutions with the aim of maintaining themselves in power for as long as possible. In

August 1996, the compliant Congress passed legislation known as 'the authentic interpretation' of the Constitution. This law consisted of just one article, which shows the depths of hypocrisy to which the Fujimori regime could sink:

> The authentic interpretation of Article 112 of the Constitution refers to presidential mandates begun at a later date than the promulgation of the aforementioned constitutional document. Consequently the authentic intepretation necessary implies that those presidential periods begun before the Constitution came into effect shall not be taken into account.

Put more simply, there was no problem about Fujimori standing for president for a third time in 2000, because his first presidency had begun before the adoption of the 1993 Constitution. Therefore, so his argument went, he was, according to the Constitution, entitled to two full consecutive terms in office from 1995 onwards.

However, the Constitutional Tribunal – an institution actually set up by the new Constitution as the highest authority on constitutional matters – ruled by three votes to nil against this new legislation. Four judges abstained. The three judges who had voted against the measure were not only sacked, but immediately became the target of a smear campaign and reprisals. The one woman judge, Delia Revoredo, and her husband were accused of such offences as illegally importing a car into Peru, and were subjected to harassment and intimidation. After their dismissal, the Constitutional Tribunal continued to debate constitutional issues, but lacked the necessary number to make its rulings binding.

Apart from this particular issue, attempts to reform Peru's judicial system, in part agreed with the World Bank as an essential component of the government's reform programme, also fell foul of the president's need to ensure that the institutions of the state would do as they were told. The first National Council for the Magistracy, set up in 1995, was intended to guarantee the independence and competence of judges and public prosecutors. By mid-1996 the council's powers to dismiss members of the judiciary found guilty of incompetence or misconduct were restricted; another law passed by Congress in 1997 gave the same authority to judges appointed provisionally (usually Fujimori supporters) as to those who held permanent positions; and then in March 1998 another law was passed limiting the council's ability to investigate allegations against any members of the Supreme Court or the state prosecution service. These powers were re-assigned to the executive.

As a result, not only did the seven members of the Council resign, but the World Bank threatened to withdraw the US$22.5-million loan promised to help the reform of Peru's judicial system. In October 1998, when the World Bank was about to cancel the loan, the Fujimori government suddenly announced that it had no need of the money anyway. The sacked Constitutional judge Delia Revoredo summed up her view of all these attacks on the judicial system: 'when the seizure of political power is gradual and begins through legislation, gradually controlling the justice system, other countries do not react as they would in the case of a coup. No one realizes, no one says anything. But bit by bit, a dictatorship is created.'[4]

A further serious abuse in the administration of justice during Fujimori's second term was the continuing reliance on military courts and 'anti-terrorist' legislation. Despite the fact that *Sendero Luminoso* had been destroyed, most of its leaders jailed and its supporters forced underground or reduced to small, insignificant groups in the interior, legislation brought in at the height of the insurgency was still regularly used throughout the country.

Special military tribunals could convict people of 'treason', while hundreds of individuals were locked up on suspicion of being 'terrorists' simply on the say-so of others. People accused in this way were not afforded proper defence and were not allowed to see the evidence being used against them. Their trials were held in secret, and there was no cross-examination of witnesses. According to Coletta Youngers of the Washington Office on Latin America, the military courts found 97 per cent of those brought before them guilty; the most common sentence passed was up to 30 years in prison, under a harsh regime that allowed only one hour a day outside the cell, with visits restricted to once every three months.[5]

The continued use of anti-terrorist legislation and special military courts was repeatedly condemned internationally both by human rights NGOs and international judicial organisations. In 1999, the Inter-American Court of Human Rights of the Organisation of American States ruled that four Chileans sentenced by a Peruvian military tribunal to life imprisonment should be retried. In response, President Fujimori announced that Peru would withdraw from membership of the Court, a decision ratified almost overnight by an obliging Congress. The Inter-American Court subsequently ruled that Peru could not unilaterally decide to withdraw from its jurisdiction; Fujimori replied that he would ignore any of the Court's rulings with regard to Peru or its citizens.

After the fall of Fujimori, one of the commissions set up to look into his government's activities investigated all the abuses against the judiciary. One of its main conclusions, published in 2001, was that: 'Alberto Fujimori intervened in the justice system, the "public ministry" and other state institutions linked to the administration of justice in order to build up a network of magistrates that would favour his politico-criminal interests: to secure presidential re-election, to guarantee his impunity, to control political opponents, and to promote the interests of third parties.'[6]

At the same time, Fujimori sought to limit the powers of Congress to act as a counterbalance to his power. From 1995 to 2000, his supporters had a clear majority, so there was little chance of any of his legislative proposals being rejected or significantly modified. In order to be sure, however, he ruled increasingly by decree, and a compliant Congress agreed that these decrees should immediately become law. According to a Ministry of Justice investigation carried out after the fall of the regime, between 1993 and July 2000 more than a thousand emergency decrees, which had the force of law, were promulgated. Significantly, a great majority of these concerned public spending, which Fujimori sought to bring under his personal control, while Montesinos was busy using the money for his own personal ends. More than US$100 million of public money was appropriated and spent in this way without Congress ever knowing about it.

Whenever opposition voices in Congress tried to protest, and to set up commissions to investigate these matters or other financial dealings undertaken by the government, or human rights issues, they were voted down. During Fujimori's second term in office, as many as 260 motions were tabled calling for the setting up of specific commissions: only six were accepted. The veteran Congressman Henry Pease complained: 'The aim was to protect those who ran the government mafia from any investigation. The effects of any accusation were diminished; there was a complete refusal to allow any investigations, or in the most extreme cases to allow only a farce instead of a real effort to uncover the truth.'[7]

With a submissive majority in Congress, and with the judicial system under control, one of the few areas of national life that could still claim independence from Fujimori in the second half of the 1990s was the mass media. This made it a target for bribery (the full extent of which only came to light with the appearance of the 'Vladivideos' in 2000–2001) and for pressure and threats when it was seen as dangerous to the regime in any way. Control of the media was so vital that the investigative journalist Gustavo Gorriti has claimed:

> Vladimiro Montesinos was the greatest unofficial editor and media owner in the history of Peru. No one has had such simultaneous control of so many media outlets; no one has decided and directed their editorial line as he did. And since he was such an enemy of journalism, the fact that he could control the media, could pervert them and use them to his advantage represented for him an even greater triumph than that of controlling and perverting the armed forces after being expelled from them for treason.[8]

Montesinos quickly realized that the most effective way of controlling the mass media was not by buying off individual journalists, but by going directly to the owners of TV channels, radio stations, and newspapers. One of the most scandalous 'Vladivideos' seen after his downfall showed exactly how he treated the Peruvian media barons. It pictured him with José Crousillat, one of the brothers who owned Canal 4, the most popular TV station. In full view of the camera, Montesinos counts out the amazing total of 1,875,000 soles (some US$600,000) in cash, and even apologises that he has not had time to change it into US dollars. He makes it plain that this is the first of regular payments, and he even has a contract on the table in front of him guaranteeing Crousillat US$1.5 million each month to help pay the station's debts. In return Canal 4 agrees not to broadcast any interviews or propaganda from any party other than Fujimori's. Further still, a clause in the contract calls on Canal 4's news programmes to 'co-ordinate and approve' each day's bulletins in advance with Montesinos.

But the deals were not just with one TV station. Ernesto Schutz of Panamerica Television (Canal 5) appears in another secret video, receiving US$350,000, part of monthly payments which Montesinos himself later claimed had totalled more than US$10 million.

Throughout Fujimori's second term, and increasingly as the 2000 elections approached, Montesinos also spent government money on setting up and backing as many as 15 cheap tabloid newspapers. Known as the *prensa chicha* (gutter press), they would carry the daily headlines for which he paid up to US$5,000. These would constantly praise the work of 'El Chino' or invent scandals involving opposition figures – often thanks to information gathered illegally by Montesinos' National Intelligence Service.

Those who refused to be bought off were dealt with in other ways. One of the most notorious cases was the treatment of Baruch Ivcher, the leading shareholder in Canal 2 TV. Ivcher, an Israeli citizen who had come to Peru in 1970, was initially a strong supporter of Fujimori, but after the 1995 re-election Canal 2 adopted an increasingly critical stance, particularly over the undisclosed role of Montesinos as the unofficial head of the National Intelligence Service.

In April 1997, Canal 2 broadcast a programme showing the alleged torture of two intelligence officers by their own colleagues. This led to uproar, but

> it was when Ivcher's company went on to show leaked tax documents that apparently showed that Montesinos' declared earnings for 1995 were almost three quarters of a million dollars (his post in the intelligence services was supposed to be unpaid) that the campaign against the TV company and its owner started in earnest.[9]

As in many other areas, the methods included using legislation and state institutions to resolve the problem. In this case, a decree was promulgated which stipulated that someone born outside Peru could not be a majority shareholder in a Peruvian media company. Although Ivcher prudently headed for Miami at this point, Canal 2 had one more shock in store for Montesinos: it aired another programme based on the illegal phone tapping operations (almost 200 of them) carried out by the intelligence services. This led to Ivcher's Peruvian nationality being rescinded, and his losing control of the company.

Other independent journalists faced threats or suddenly found their contracts cancelled. In their book *The Imperfect Spy*, Sally Bowen and Jane Holligan report that one journalist was sent a chicken's head through the post to deter her from investigating the La Cantuta killings, while another investigative reporter received several death threats by telephone.[10] Almost all journalists who had not been bought off had their phones tapped and their movements followed.

At the same time as he was masterminding these efforts to perpetuate Fujimori and himself in power, Montesinos continued to pile up millions of dollars in illegal deals. One of the most scandalous concerned the purchase of aircraft from Eastern Europe. With tension still running high in 1996 because of the border situation with Ecuador, the Peruvian air force was seeking to strengthen its capacity. As during the earlier conflict, Montesinos saw in this problem the perfect opportunity to make money. According to the testimony of one of his associates, Victor Alberto Venero, Montesinos set up a company, w-21 Intertechnique, in Panama with a group of his most trusted friends (allegedly with initial capital of only US$5,000). They then approached several governments in Eastern Europe for hardware to buy. Montesinos and the others were to be paid a lavish commission for their efforts.

After a failed attempt to buy aircraft from the Ukraine, the group settled on Belarus. The deal was to buy 18 MIG-29 and

SU-25 warplanes. The total cost of the aircraft and maintenance, radar and missile systems was in excess of US$470
million – quite a bill for a company with only a few thousand
dollars capital. The money to pay for all this came from the
funds produced by earlier privatisations, channelled to
Montesinos and his friends thanks to secret decrees that
circumvented the normal processes laid out for military
purchases. And because the top brass of the air force and
other services had already been bought off, they did not
investigate the price being asked by the Belarus authorities for
their second-hand planes: the higher the price, the higher the
commission everyone in on the deal would receive.

In this way, Montesinos used the money from privatisation
for his own personal gain. Referring to this case, Manuel
Dammert says,

> From the start the aim was to acquire illicit gains. It has been
> shown that no less than $60 million were paid in illegal commis-
> sions. With regard to Montesinos alone, the existence in a Swiss
> bank account of $48 million in his name has been confirmed,
> and a further $12 million which, according to Venero, he paid
> him in cash as part of the 'toll' he demanded for the Belarus
> deal.[11]

The deal itself turned out to be a mixed blessing. One of
the Belarus MIGs crashed soon after purchase, and another
failed spectacularly in 2001. As many as eight of the SU-25s
could not be flown, while maintenance and spare parts for
the fleet proved a constant problem.

In this case as in many others, it proved simple for Montesinos to bypass all checks on government spending. In part
this was due to confusion over how much had actually come
into the government coffers with privatisation.

Alberto Fujimori has always denied responsibility for any
of these illegal deals. As this book went to press, the cases

against him had not got as far as those for which Montesinos is facing trial. During his second term, Fujimori still promoted himself as the honest, hard-working Oriental. 'Work itself, the daily bustle, is what keeps me going. That, a balanced diet and contact with the poor of Peru', he told reporters in 1996. His victory in the 1995 elections helped to legitimise his rule internationally, and he began to travel abroad more frequently in search of foreign investment and to defend his government. When he came to London in 1998, he took lunch with the Queen and was received with great pomp in the splendour of Lancaster House. His efforts at modernising Peru were warmly praised by politicians and top businessmen, who were all impressed by his painstaking English. He answered questions from human rights groups with apparent frankness, arguing that he had succeeded in putting an end to terrorism without using too draconian measures. Outside the palace where he was feted, there were only four demonstrators.

But while Montesinos turned the state into a vast money-making machine, Fujimori manipulated it for personal power. He concentrated spending in social areas – education, health and so on – in his Ministry of the Presidency. This served a double purpose. On the one hand, it drained money and therefore influence from other ministries. On the other hand, whatever was achieved was then directly attributable to his own efforts, and helped to cement his position in power. His initiatives in the social sector often had disastrous consequences, as in the mass sterilisation campaign that he vigorously promoted from 1995 onwards.

One of the most surprising delegates at the United Nations Fourth World Conference on Women in Beijing in 1995 had been none other than Alberto Fujimori. When he returned to Peru, he immediately started to put his new-found enthusiasm for women's rights into effect. On 25 July 1995 he launched his government's new reproductive rights and family planning programme. 'We always have been and always will be a pragmatic government with no taboos or "sacred cows",' he told journalists. 'The women of Peru must be in charge of their own destinies.'

This new initiative was followed in September 1995 with an amendment to the constitutional law on population. This was to allow surgical means of birth control – banned under a law passed in the 1970s. The aim, according to Fujimori, was to allow all those women who so desired to have access to free sterilisation. This move was attacked by the Catholic Church, which condemns all artificial methods of birth control, but was given backing inside Peru by women's groups such as 'Flora Tristan' and others, and received international funds and training support from the US Agency for International Development (USAID) and the UN Population Fund (UNFPA).

According to Giulia Tamayo of the Latin American Women's Development Centre (*Centro Latinoamericano de Desarrollo de la Mujer* – CLADEM), who was one of the first to denounce the scandal in 1998:

> The campaign was based on good principles. The argument was that large families were one of the causes of poverty, and that therefore there was a need to increase awareness of family planning. In Peru, the national average is 3.5 children per woman, and this average rises to 5.6 in rural areas. So an educational campaign was essential.[12]

But she goes on to put her finger on what went wrong with the Fujimori government's good intentions: 'When in 1996 it became legal to perform sterilisations, the authorities no longer bothered about educational niceties, but went straight to the operation. And in an authoritarian country like Peru, what happened was bound to happen.'[11]

What happened was that in order to please the president – who was reportedly kept informed each month of the figures – the health ministry set targets for the number of surgical operations to be carried out in order to bring the birth rate down. What had started out as targets very quickly became quotas to be filled, by any means. And so the campaign soon had little to do with women deciding how many children they wanted, but became one of forced sterilisation, carried out especially in the poorer regions of the Andes, the Amazon basin, and the shanty towns around the edges of Lima. In 1996, almost 82,000 women of child-bearing age had their tubes tied; in 1997 the figure rose to some 130,000. Altogether the government programme led to more than 330,000 sterilisations between 1995 and the fall of the Fujimori government in 2000.

There were even special 'tube-tying' fiestas organised, with dancing, games, fun for all the family, and a free operation for the mothers, many of whom had only the vaguest idea of what they were submitting to. In some areas, in order to achieve the quota, women were offered money (the usual figure was said to be 100 soles, around US$55 at the time) or gifts of food. In highland areas, many women were sterilised without their knowledge when they were in hospital for another problem. An investigation carried out in Ayacucho province, after the scandal became public, discovered health officials' memos which stated: 'Objectives: to promote the use of irreversible contraceptive methods. Incentives for the group: 15 kilos of food. Special prize for personnel carrying out the greatest number of fallopian tubes tied: trip for three people to any destination in the country.'

It was in 1998 that the first questions about the sterilisation campaign began to be asked in the Peruvian press. In particular, the Lima daily *El Comercio* carried a report on 22 June 1998 from a reporter who had been shocked at the treatment of women in the poor highland areas near Cuzco. The report spoke of the 'many deaths caused by negligence, poor hygiene, lack of proper training among the medical staff, and a lack of regard for the general health of the patients …'. This investigation, as well as others carried out by foreign funding agencies, led to the sterilisation campaign being quickly wound down. But this time President Fujimori said nothing, and no one offered an apology to the women who had been operated on. According to a post-Fujimori ministry of health report (July 2002) 'the vast majority of them were forced into the operation, either by pressure or threats, or in return for payments or food donations, without the consequences being properly explained to them. This prevented them from making any kind of informed choice.'

Opposition to President Fujimori during his second term in office was at first splintered and ineffective, while the president was undoubtedly still popular with a substantial majority of Peruvians. It was not many months, however, before the limits of his political power were made clear. In November 1995 there were elections for mayors throughout Peru. The two most important were those in the capital, Lima, and in the nearby port of Callao. Fujimori and his team were anxious to win these posts, but in both cases the government candidates were soundly beaten.

As usual, dirty tricks took over where honest politics had failed. The central government starved Lima's new mayor, Alberto Andrade, of the funds he needed to implement change, while the mayor of Callao, Alex Kouri, was eventually bought off. But these reverses were important because they convinced Fujimori and Montesinos that their stay in power depended directly on the figure of the president. It was probably at this moment that they and the others in the close-knit group of advisers round them began to devote an increasing amount of time, energy and money to ensuring that the way was open for Fujimori to stand for a third term in elections due to be held in 2000. This in turn helped to unite the fragmented opposition and give a clear focus to its protests and campaigns.

Grassroots organisations had suffered greatly during the long years of civil conflict. On the one hand, any attempts to organise to press for economic or social improvement were regarded by the army as subversive. On the other hand, *Sendero Luminoso* in particular wanted to control any such initiatives, and those that it could not infiltrate or influence were attacked. An especially vicious example of this was the assassination of María Elena Moyano, deputy mayor of the shanty town Villa El Salvador to the south of Lima.

Originally founded early in the 1970s by some 10,000 migrants from the Huaraz area, by the 1990s more than a quarter of a million people were living in the Villa. What distinguished Villa El Salvador from other shanty towns was the level of community participation and organisation, which made it a prime target for *Sendero*, as the feminist writer Virginia Vargas has explained:

> the popular nature of feminist organisations like the one in Villa El Salvador, their democratic spirit, and the clear rejection they made of the use of violence and terror, as well as their dedication to the daily struggle to overcome the difficulties arising from the country's economic crisis, are some of the reasons why they were anathema to *Sendero's* political interests.[13]

In February 1992, Moyano was shot dead by *Sendero* members in front of her two young children 'as a warning to others'. When the mayor of the town protested, he too was shot and wounded.

This violence against any popular organisation was repeated throughout Peru, in particular in the highland regions, where the struggle between the authorities and the insurgent groups was at its fiercest. The great insecurity in itself led ordinary people to withdraw from participation in grassroots activities, a process encouraged by the massive privatisation of state concerns and the concomitant growth of the 'black economy', where everyone had to look after their own interests. The trade unions were also affected by this process, and were further weakened by their doctrinaire positions in resisting change without offering any viable alternatives.

At the same time, President Fujimori co-opted existing groups and turned them into government-run programmes, which then came to depend on his generosity to remain effective. This was the case for the National Food Aid Programme (PRONAA), which by 1998 was absorbing as much as 25 per cent of the government's total budget.[14] According to a survey in 2000, this programme was providing no less than 10 million Peruvians with some or all of their daily food. But this aid did not come without strings attached. During the 1995 election campaign, the women from the kitchens receiving the food were required to attend government rallies, while by 1998 they were told they should wear orange (the official colour) caps and aprons. If they did not, there was an implicit and sometimes explicit threat that government aid would be cut.

Despite all this, opposition to the Fujimori regime grew steadily during his second period in office. One group included many of those who had been directly affected by the years of violence. As the 2003 Truth and Reconciliation Report showed, nearly 70,000 people lost their lives in the struggle, while as many as 600,000 Peruvians were displaced by it.

The longer the Fujimori government took to resolve their problems, or even to admit that thousands of ordinary Peruvians had 'disappeared', the more inclined these people were to become opponents of the regime.

They were often helped by Catholic church organisations. As in Chile, a *Vicaria de la Solidaridad* was set up in many regions of Peru, to attend to the basic needs of the victims of violence, and to allow them to organise in search of justice. In Ayacucho, relatives of those who had disappeared were encouraged to tell their stories, while support groups attempted to give comfort and support. As in many Latin American countries, the Catholic church in Peru was split between a conservative hierarchy and a more progressive ordinary clergy. Fujimori's initial closeness to the protestant evangelical sects and his promotion of family planning also made the Catholic church authorities wary of him.

In addition to the efforts of the church, resistance to Fujimori's policies was often led by the NGOs, many of them financed by foreign money. The imprisonment of 'innocents' – the hundreds of people tried by military court and sentenced to long periods in jail simply as a result of accusations by others – became a focal point for NGOs, and the *Coordinadora Nacional de Derechos Humanos* (National Human Rights Coordinating Body) began a campaign on their behalf. The response to this campaign among ordinary Peruvians showed that they were beginning to lose their fear of being accused in their turn of 'supporting terrorism', and brought increasing pressure for the proper rule of law.

Pressure on this issue within Peru and internationally led to the setting up of the Ad Hoc Commission to investigate the cases of those imprisoned for 'terrorism' who maintained their innocence. By the end of 1999, when the work of the Commission was declared complete, 481 Peruvians had been granted a presidential pardon, and several hundred more had been freed by the courts. There was another long battle to ensure that those released in this way had their criminal records destroyed, but claims for compensation for loss of earnings during their false imprisonment were never settled.

The first issue to bring together the varied opposition groups – the NGOs, political parties, grassroots organisations and students alike – was the 1996 protest at the 'authentic interpretation' by Fujimori supporters in Congress, by which the president would be allowed to stand again in the elections due in 2000, as he had been elected only once under the terms of the 1993 Constitution.

The opposition gathered in what was baptised the *Foro Democrático*, which applied to the electoral tribunal to try to collect some 1.4 million signatures (10 per cent of the electorate) and force a referendum on whether Fujimori could be a candidate again. As Alejandra Alayza, a leader of the student movement at the time, recalls:

> the campaign against the Law of Amnesty and the Referendum were important because this was the first time that students felt they could re-occupy a public space. They had lived through the worst violence, and now communication between different universities started again, and students felt that they could take to the streets again and make the voice of students heard on a political issue of national significance.[14]

It took two years to complete the collection of signatures, but then, as on so many other occasions, the regime changed the rules to defeat this popular initiative.

First the election board ruled that a law passed after the start of the signatures campaign had begun could be applied retroactively. This law stipulated that for a popular referendum to be held on any topic, in addition to a sufficient number of signatures, the proposal had to win the support of two-fifths of the members of Congress. In this case, the referendum idea was put to Congress for debate during a late-night sitting on 27 August 1998, and defeated by the compliant majority. Although these tactics led to mass protests in several cities, *Foro Democrático* had to admit defeat, and turned its energies to the 2000 elections themselves.

As the time for the elections approached, President Fujimori still seemed to be in an almost unbeatable position. On the external front, he had put an end to the conflict with neighbouring Ecuador by signing a peace deal – although many Peruvians felt he had been too generous in the terms of the agreement, which offered Ecuador in theory at least a route out to the Atlantic down the Amazon, and gave them some territorial concessions. At home, although economic growth had slowed considerably, and his plans for privatisation of more sectors of the economy had run into trouble, he could still play the card of having defeated terrorism (as with the ending of the siege in the Japanese ambassador's residence – see box p. 67) and having rid most of the country of violence.

This time, though, he faced several strong opponents. One was the popular mayor of the capital, Alberto Andrade and his Somos Peru party; another was Luis Castañeda Lossio, who was thought to have done a good job when he had been health minister, and there was the former shoe-shine boy who had been sponsored to study economics in the United States, Alejandro Toledo, who revived his *Peru Posible* political grouping. As on previous occasions, Fujimori and Montesinos marshalled all the resources of the state to ensure that the 'president-candidate' would win re-election. The ministry of the presidency offered more schools, roads, and other infrastructure projects. The soup kitchens and *vaso de leche* (cup of milk) programmes became increasingly political, with their members 'encouraged' to support Fujimori at rallies and at the ballot. The TV and radio stations that had been bought off by the government refused to accept any electoral propaganda from the opposition candidates, while Montesinos mounted a vicious smear campaign against Toledo, Andrade and the others.

The opposition cried foul, and so did international observers. The Carter Foundation (set up by former US President Jimmy Carter in Atlanta) sent a team to observe the election campaign, and they concluded that the government was unfairly using its privileged position for media access; that the media were providing unfair and biased reports on opposition candidates, who were also suffering direct harassment; that the electoral authorities should prove to the electorate's satisfaction that they were impartial, and should allow outside observers free access to all areas of the voting process.

Peruvian opposition groups meanwhile filed 18 different legal motions with the electoral authorities arguing that Fujimori was ineligible to stand again. The National Election Board rejected all the motions out of hand. The many different civil groups then decided to concentrate their attention on making sure that the first round of voting in April 2000 was as fair as possible. Thousands of observers were enrolled by the Transpariencia group, who checked electoral rolls for fraud, protested if opposition candidates were not allowed access to the media, and signed up to monitor polling on the day of the election.

Increasingly, the struggle of the opposition groups became an effort to ensure that Fujimori and Montesinos did not manipulate the vote to give 'el Chino' victory in the first round. It was felt that in much the same way as he had come from behind to beat Mario Vargas Llosa a decade earlier, this time round his own vote would peak in April, while all those who did not want him to continue would get behind a single candidate in the run-off election, scheduled for the end of May. As election day drew nearer, a rumour started flying around: that Montesinos was organising a coup, which would get rid of Fujimori and replace him with someone who could be sold as more 'democratic' and in tune with the new Peru, but who would follow the same basic policies and continue

Siege and Slaughter

On 17 December 1996, members of the *Movimiento Revolu-cionario Tupac Amaru* (MRTA) burst into a reception at the Japanese ambassador's residence. They took hostage many members of the government, including foreign minister Francisco Tudela and Fujimori's younger brother Pedro, together with prominent foreign diplomats and others. The siege lasted for four months, with negotiations dragging on without apparently achieving anything, until on the afternoon of 22 April 1997, commandos emerged from tunnels dug underneath the residence, killed all 14 MRTA rebels and rescued the hostages. Fujimori himself was soon on the scene, claiming what the army called the 'Chavin de Huantar' operation as his personal triumph. But while it is true that opinion polls showed that his popularity soared after the successful rescue, a significant number of Peruvians saw this as a crucial example of the government's willingness to use force rather than legal means to resolve conflicts. This incident underlined how much the regime depended on Fujimori and his closest associates, and at the same time acted as a spur to opponents to organise to try to find a different way to resolve problems of this sort.

the alliance with the armed forces and the security services.

On polling day itself, there were hundreds of protests, but little violence. And when the counting of the votes was finished a few days later, an extraordinary result emerged. President Fujimori was given 49.9 per cent of the vote, just 0.1 per cent short of outright victory. The main opposition contender turned out to be Alejandro Toledo – like Fujimori in 1990, a political outsider who had been thought only a few months earlier to have little chance of making any impact, but ended by winning 40 per cent of first-round votes cast.

The Lovely Laura Bozzo

Nobody was a clearer product of the Fujimori–Montesinos regime than the Channel 4 talk show host Laura Bozzo. A glamorous dyed-blonde, she fronted a show that was a mixture of Jerry Springer and Oprah Winfrey, in which couples fought and denounced each other in terms never seen or heard before on Peruvian television. Her performances became the most popular programme on TV, and were shown every day. Sally Bowen and Jane Holligan recall one show, called 'What would you do for money?', in which a female member of the audience was persuaded to lick the sweat from a man's armpits for the princely reward of US$10.[15] But Bozzo was also important politically. She would often underline her support for the government, and at Montesinos' prompting would invite on to the show guests whose stories could harm opposition candidates. It was she who presented to Peruvians Toledo's unacknowledged daughter, born out of wedlock; she questioned whether a man who would not recognise his own child was worthy of anyone's vote. After the regime collapsed, Bozzo was arrested on suspicion of having been paid US$3 million by Montesinos from illegal funds.

Although the opposition was relieved that Fujimori had been denied re-election, the protests still continued. There were calculations that the government had committed fraud worth about 10 per cent of the total ballots. The team sent by the OAS spoke of many serious failings. On 25 April, US President Bill Clinton warned that economic, political and military ties with Peru would be affected unless there was a free and fair second round. Fujimori emphasised his support for the democratic process, and promised to respect whatever the popular verdict was.

Denunciations of fraud continued for weeks after the first round, and the same abuses and manipulation was all too evident in the lead-up to the run-off vote. Once again, the electoral authorities showed how partial they were by dismissing the allegations of fraud and refusing to postpone the second round while they were dealt with.

A few weeks before the vote, Alejandro Toledo decided to pull out, arguing that the election was fraudulent and that to accept it would make him an accomplice in Fujimori's machinations. Unsurprisingly, the electoral authorities said that his withdrawal had come too late to halt the electoral process, and the second round duly went ahead on 28 May. The international observers who had been present in April refused to sanction the voting with their presence. Abstention rates were high, and almost a third of those who did vote spoiled their ballots either by voting for Toledo or scrawling 'no to fraud' on their ballot papers. However, Alberto Fujimori was officially declared the winner, with some 74 per cent of the valid votes cast in his favour, although his opponents argued that after all the abstentions and the spoilt papers were added together, he had still won the support of only a minority of the voters.

Although Fujimori had officially been re-elected for a third term in office, the protests did not die down. Inside Peru, organisations such as the human rights group *Instituto de Defensa Legal* (IDEELE) christened this a 'Frankenstein election' and listed 830 irregularities, which, they said, meant that neither round of voting had been free or fair. Abroad, the OAS and the United States both called for the Fujimori regime to talk to opposition representatives in an attempt to ensure 'democratic rule'. Alejandro Toledo still campaigned, claiming to have been the real victor at the polls.

A huge march from the four corners of Peru – the *marcha de los cuatro suyos* – was organised to coincide with Fujimori's third swearing-in on 28 July. When he received the sash of office, it was in a presidential palace surrounded by troops and armed police, who were trying to keep away the million demonstrators who had converged on the capital to express their anger and rejection of the political farce being played out at the seat of power. But despite this huge protest, and the deaths of six people among the protesters, Peru seemed set for five more years of rule by a tiny authoritarian group concerned only with perpetuating themselves in power. It was only a few months, however, before the Fujimori–Montesinos regime finally came tumbling down.

Notes

1. Sally Bowen, *The Fujimori File*, Peru Monitor, Lima, 2000, p. 227.
2. *El Comercio*, Lima, 10 April 1995.
3. *El Comercio*, Lima, 11 April 1995.
4. Bowen, op. cit., p. 282.
5. Colette Youngers, *Deconstructing Democracy: Peru under Fujimori*, Washington Office on Latin America, Washington, 2000, p. 39.
6. Congreso de la República del Peru, *Informe final de la comisión especial de la investigación sobre los delitos cometidos entre 1990–2000*, Lima, 2002.
7. Henry Pease, interview with authors, April 2004.
8. Gustavo Gorriti, interview with authors, April 2004.
9. Sally Bowen and Jane Holligan, *The Imperfect Spy: The Many Lives of Vladimiro Montesinos*, Peisa, Lima, 2003, p. 312.
10. Manuel Dammert, *Fujimori–Montesinos, el estado mafioso*, Ediciones El Virrey, Lima, 2001, p. 216.
11. Giulia Tamayo, *Le Monde Diplomatique*, May 2004, pp. 14–15.
12. Virginia Vargas, 'Women: Tragic Encounters with the Left', NACLA *Report on the Americas*, Vol. 25, 1992, p. 46.
13. Claude Auroi and Sandra Bossio (eds), *A donde va el Perú?*, Institut Universitaire d'Etudes du Développement, Cuzco, 2002, p. 42.
14. Alexandra Alayza, interview with authors, April 2004.
15. Bowen and Holligan, op. cit., p. 331.

4
A Fresh Start

Even though Alberto Fujimori had succeeded in his aim of being elected for a third time, his hold on power in July 2000 was weaker than at any point in the previous decade. More Peruvians than ever before had come out on to the streets to demonstrate against the regime. Many civil society organisations were repeatedly questioning the shady deals and corruption already evident in the *Fujimorato*. Peruvian business and financial circles were worried about the general atmosphere of instability and uncertainty. And internationally, the plethora of irregularities during both rounds of the elections had led people to distance themselves from Fujimori, which meant the loss of several strands of foreign aid.

There was a widespread sense that the regime could not last, although few Peruvians foresaw the spectacular way in which it would collapse. Even before the elections, *El Comercio* newspaper had raised questions about Montesinos yet again, giving details of bank balances showing that he held accounts worth several million dollars – not bad for someone who was supposedly giving his time and talents for free. Then, at the end of August 2000, just as the government was supposed to be starting talks with the opposition and OAS representatives on making Peru more truly democratic, the question of the sale of arms to left-wing guerrillas in Colombia came to light.

At first Montesinos and Fujimori claimed that they had

successfully dismantled a ring using Peru to smuggle Kalashnikov rifles bought in Jordan to the Colombian Revolutionary Armed Forces (FARC). Gradually, though, a very different story came to light. What had really happened, it transpired, was that Montesinos had seen the chance to make a few more million dollars through parachuting some 10,000 Russian AK-47 rifles to the insurgents in the south of Colombia through third parties, who would be paid in cocaine. As usual, he had bought off the Peruvian armed forces, and arranged for the transport planes to land either in the jungle town of Iquitos or in Lima. Altogether, he is thought to have made more than US$7 million on the deal. Unfortunately for him, somewhere along the line the CIA got wind of the transactions, and for whatever reasons decided that this might be a good opportunity to get rid of Montesinos. In desperation, he seems to have concocted the idea of the Peruvian intelligence services discovering the affair and successfully putting a stop to it. The FARC themselves called this 'a fairy tale'.

There were also more directly political scandals, and it was one of these that led to the downfall of the 'Siamese twins'. After the first round of the elections in April 2000, NGOs such as Transparency International began to question whether Peru 2000, the political group backing Fujimori, had in fact succeeded in collecting the million signatures necessary to give it the right to stand as a political party. As scrutiny of the signatures began, it became clear that Fujimori had gone back to his roots – his family and others had got together and forged several hundred thousand signatures of supposed 'supporters' of the group.

There was a further surprise when the 120 members of Congress came to be sworn in. Twelve of those who had stood for other political groupings now declared that they supported Fujimori's *Alianza Electoral Peru 2000* (made up of *Vamos Vecino, Cambio 90* and *Nueva Mayoría*). This gave the government a clear majority of seats, meaning business as usual for Fujimori and Montesinos. A sign of how far the traditional parties had lost ground since the return to civilian rule in 1980 was the fact that almost all the members of Congress came from new groupings such as *Peru Posible* (Toledo), the *Frente Independiente Moralizador* (FIM), led by Fernando Olivera, Somos Peru and the *Partido Aprista* Peruano (PAP). Many of the most established parties, such as the PSUC and even APRA, had been all but wiped out, although many of their members had transferred allegiance to the new forces.

But it was the dismay at how Fujimori had yet again made a mockery of democratic rules that brought him down. Amidst continuing protests, someone in Montesinos' entourage, encouraged by the increasingly worried intelligence services, passed the first, fatal 'Vladivideo' to Fernando Olivera. One irony of the situation was that after the tens of millions of dollars which Montesinos had stolen, and all the illegal deals he and the president had struck over their ten years in power, this first video showed him bribing a politician with the measly sum of US$15,000. This was all it took for the opposition politician Alberto Kouri to throw his political principles out of the window and join the government party after the 2000 elections.

In fact, as more and more of the videos filmed in Montesinos' 'sitting-room' in the National Intelligence Headquarters came to light, it was plain that he was an expert judge as to exactly how much money it would take to buy a person's allegiance: TV station owners and generals were doled out millions of dollars, others received no more than a few thousand. The effect, however, was the same – from then on, they were in Montesinos' debt, and he could call in the favour whenever it suited him.

This dramatic first video was shown on Thursday 14

September 2000. On Saturday 16 September Fujimori addressed the country on TV and radio. He told a stunned nation that he was accepting responsibility for what had happened – although what had been revealed at that point was only the tiny tip of a monstrous iceberg – and that as a result he was not only dismantling the National Intelligence Service, but was calling fresh presidential and congressional elections for the following April, in which he would not stand. As the news that he was stepping down filtered out, thousands of people began collecting in Lima's main square outside the presidential palace, calling for him to go immediately. There was little violence, and many in the square had by now become sufficiently wary of 'El Chino's' pronouncements to know that there was a huge difference between his announcing something and his actually carrying out his promises.

This state of tension lasted for several days, with many Peruvians fearing that Montesinos' friends in the cupola of the armed forces would stage a coup to keep him in power, and President Fujimori still vacillating and undecided after his announcement. It was not until Montesinos was on his way to exile in Panama, with a governmental endorsement 'recognising his participation in counter-subversive successes, in fighting drug-trafficking and in achieving peace with Ecuador', and an estimated US$17 million from Ministry of Defence funds as a payoff for 'important services rendered to the nation' (or to buy his silence), that the situation became clearer.

By then Fujimori was negotiating with the opposition and with members of the OAS how to organise an orderly retreat from power. Many Congress members of Peru 2000 resigned their seats, making his government's position even more difficult. Even so, it seemed that his main political challenger, Alejandro Toledo, and other leading political figures were willing to go along with the timetable he had set for new elections, and the measures he offered to put in place to make sure that this time they were truly free and fair. One of the main sticking points to agreement was the president and the armed forces' insistence that there should be another general amnesty declared before they quit power, so that they would not have to face any trials in the future.

Once again, it was Montesinos himself who upset the precarious political balance. Although Panama had often received the most unsavoury characters from Latin America and the Caribbean, and although its banking and financial systems had traditionally welcomed money from whatever source, by the start of the new millennium things were changing even there. President Mireya Moscoso came under great pressure from Washington and other Latin American leaders not to grant Montesinos permanent exile, so that by mid-October Montesinos felt it was unsafe to stay there. Perhaps thinking that he could benefit from the general amnesty if it was passed in Peru, he made his way secretly back to Lima.

Days of farce followed. President Fujimori put on his leather hunting jacket and led army patrols 'in search of' his former intelligence chief. At the same time, he ordered a search of the Montesinos family home. As well as some 1,500 Christian Dior shirts, 120 French and Italian suits, and several jewel-encrusted watches, the police removed almost 70 suitcases of videos that Montesinos had taken in the SIN headquarters, along with other possibly incriminating evidence. Fujimori and his close allies spent three days combing through all this, presumably removing anything that linked the president directly to his 'Siamese twin's' crimes. By the time the suitcases were handed over to the Attorney General's office, there were thirty fewer of them.

At the start of November came the final blow for Montesinos. Justice minister Alberto Bustamente revealed that the Swiss authorities had traced three bank accounts, with a total of some US$48 million in them, back to him. According to President Fujimori, it was only at this point that he grasped the full extent of his associate's corruption, and it may have been at this moment that he decided to abandon his plans to oversee the transition to elections and proper democratic rule. For his part, Montesinos plainly decided that discretion was the better part of valour, and he escaped once again from Peru, this time on board a yacht perhaps appropriately named *Karisma*, eventually reaching Venezuela.

With such confusion at the highest levels of government, Congress took on the pivotal role it had not enjoyed for years. Although Fujimori's supporters had won one last victory in October by rejecting calls for Montesinos' arrest on the basis of the videos he had taped in the SIN headquarters, the Fujimori regime was crumbling fast. After further videos had come to light showing the heads of the Peruvian armed forces receiving money – and orders – from Montesinos, they were all dismissed on 28 October. Attempts were also started to reform the judiciary: the attorney general Blanca Nelida Colán Maguinho was ousted. A special prosecutor, José Ugaz, was appointed to investigate Montesinos' affairs, and all his assets were frozen.

On 10 November, the date for fresh elections without Fujimori was officially set as 8 April 2001. On 13 November, Fujimori left for a meeting of the Asia–Pacific Economic Co-operation (APEC) in Brunei. A week later, he telephoned prime minister Federico Salas to say that he would not be coming back, and confirmed his resignation in a fax from Japan on Monday 21 November. In the meantime, the prime minister and all the cabinet had resigned, and the armed forces had issued a statement saying that they would respect the constitution and stay out of politics.

On the same day, 21 November 2000, the Congress voted by 62 votes to 9 (almost all the government coalition was apparently too scared to make an appearance) that President Fujimori was 'permanently morally unfit' for office, and was therefore stripped of the presidency. This passed the next day to the newly elected speaker of Congress, the veteran *Acción Popular* politician Valentín Paniagua, who was sworn in the following day. Although his party held only three seats in Congress at the time, he was accepted as an honest broker who could head a caretaker administration until a new constitutionally elected president could be sworn in during July 2001.

Small, plump and bespectacled, the 64-year-old Paniagua looked more like a school headmaster than a politician occupying, however briefly, the highest office in Peru. He seemed ill at ease in the French-style finery of the presidential palace, and readily admitted that 'there's little I can do to change Peru' in the eight months he was to be in power. He was very insistent that his caretaker government should above all ensure economic stability and the organisation of genuinely free elections, respecting the timetable that Fujimori himself had set.

At the same time, there was no great change of tack in economic policy: the privatisation programme, apart from the scheme to privatise Peru's ports, was allowed to continue despite the widespread protests it had generated, although an investigation was begun to find out what had happened to the proceeds from the sale of almost ninety companies which had already been sold off, often in the most dubious circumstances. Internationally, the new government accepted the levels of debt inherited from the Fujimori era, but renegotiated debt payments and reached agreement with the IMF and other multinational lending agencies to ensure their continuing support. There was also a determined effort to bring more transparency to the government's economic dealings, with consistent attempts to explain how and where state spending was going.

President Paniagua brought back as prime minister Javier Pérez de Cuellar, the man who had been soundly defeated by Fujimori in the 1995 elections, and formed a cabinet from members of the four main parties and other 'notables' who had been prominent in the struggle against Fujimori, including Diego Sayán as minister of justice, and Susana Villarán de la Puente, one of the authors of this book. Villarán was a former head of the National Human Rights Commission, who was brought in as minister for women and human development. Worried about their own political survival, Fujimori's supporters in Congress did not try to block these appointments.

From the outset, President Paniagua and his ministers saw it as essential to try to restore ordinary Peruvians' faith in their country's institutions. They immediately set about righting some of the more glaring injustices committed by the previous regime: the three members of the Constitutional Tribunal sacked by Fujimori were reinstated, as were more than 100 career diplomats sacked by Fujimori after the 1992 coup. New electoral authorities were appointed to ensure that the next elections were free and fair. Beyond these immediate measures, the government also set about clearing out corrupt state officials, judges, police, and members of the armed forces at all levels.

The atmosphere during the months of the Paniagua administration was extraordinary. The Congress building, in the heart of the old historic centre of Lima, was filled every day not only with politicians, but also journalists and members of the public. They were all anxious to see the latest revelations in the hundreds more 'Vladivideos' being viewed by a special commission to see what evidence could be gleaned from them that could lead to prosecution. As each new person from the political, judicial, or armed forces' establishment was seen to have been filmed taking a bribe, currying favour, or directly plotting with Montesinos, the stupefaction and anger increased. In other rooms of Congress, the Waisman Commission, which was charged with detailing the former leaders' corruption, was busy trying to track down the hundreds of millions of dollars that the former strongman and the president had salted away in banks from the Cayman Islands to Switzerland.

Away from Congress, strenuous efforts were made to clear out corrupt officials, and to bring them to justice if possible. The attorney-general was replaced, as was the head of the Supreme Court, and in May 2001 some 25 judges were sacked. In the armed forces, 12 generals were retired, the chief of general staff was replaced, and before long a dozen generals arrested and put in prison to await trial, as were a number of the top officers in the national police force. Some 500 bank accounts were frozen while their owners were investigated to see if the money came from illegal dealings. A national anti-corruption campaign, the Instituto Nacional Anti-corrupción (INA) was set up, which included a telephone 'corruption hotline', which in the early months of 2001 received more than 200 calls a day from ordinary citizens alleging all kinds of abuses of power.

These attempts to clean up the state and convince ordinary Peruvians that there were still honest politicians and officials in the country were all the more remarkable because Montesinos himself was still on the loose. There were wide-spread fears that he could still manipulate enough people to bring all this process of renovation crashing down. Yet another of the Paniagua government's priorities was to track him down and bring him back to Peru to face prosecution. These efforts were crowned with success in June 2001, when

Montesinos' Hidden Treasures

When the police raided the family apartment of Montesinos and his wife in Lima in November 2000 – looking mainly for any videotapes that might incriminate President Fujimori – they discovered how some at least of the millions he had stolen from the Peruvian state had been spent. They found as many as 1,500 Christian Dior shirts, and one million dollars' worth of jewellery, including several jewel-encrusted watches. His official income was calculated by the government to be just US$370 a month.

On a later raid of his beach property in Chorrillos, to the south of the capital, they found it was lavishly decorated, with an indoor swimming pool, gold filigree wallpaper and other expensive (if garish) details. But they also found that underneath a large pink bathtub, the former unofficial head of Peru's intelligence services had installed an escape tunnel leading into the street outside, just in case he had to make a quick getaway.

In their search of the SIN's headquarters after Montesinos' flight, the police made a more disturbing discovery. Underneath the rooms where he had made video recordings of all those he had had dealings with, several underground cells were found. Although several people had given evidence of being held and tortured in these 'torture dungeons', the authorities had always maintained that they did not exist.

the Interior Minister Ketín Vidal triumphantly brought the disgraced former intelligence chief back from where he had been hiding in Venezuela. He was taken to the maximum security prison at the Callao naval base – ironically, to installations he himself had designed to hold Abimael Guzmán and other high-ranking members of the armed rebel groups.

Another important consideration in the months of the transitional government was the fact that none of its members were to stand in the upcoming elections. This gave them much greater moral authority, but was also a severely limiting factor, as they knew that whatever initiatives they set in train would be dependent on the willingness of whoever won those elections to carry them through to fruition.

In the early months of 2001, there was renewed optimism and enthusiasm for the political process. Peruvians were rightly proud that they had contributed to the downfall of an autocratic and corrupt regime, and were looking to the presidential and congressional candidates to continue with change and renewal to make sure that the hijacking of the Peruvian state by a small group of determined, unscrupulous individuals could not happen again.

Every effort was made to ensure that this time the elections were not only fair but seen to be fair. The renewed electoral authorities welcomed national and international supervision, and hundreds of volunteers were enrolled to check that there was as little fraud as possible in the polling stations. The OAS and the European Union, who had been so critical of the 2000 elections, this time gave their approval for the way the run-up to the voting and events on the day itself were carried out.

The frontrunner throughout the campaign was Alejandro Toledo and his *Peru Posible* party. Toledo had emerged as the person behind whom all the anti-Fujimori forces had rallied in 2000, and his popularity continued this time, despite persistent rumours that he too figured in several 'Vladivideos' and the fact that he offered few concrete proposals. His chief rivals were Lourdes Flores Nano, the leader of the right-wing *Alianza Unidad Nacional*, whose political programme was a more honest version of the Fujimori years, and a surprising third figure. This was none other than the former president,

---

La Cuculiza and the Giraffes

One example of the scale of corruption that had taken place under Fujimori that caught the public imagination was the story of the minister for women and the giraffes that never reached Lima. When Susana Villarán was appointed Minister for Women and Human Development in the transitional government, she found one of her more unusual responsibilities was for the Lima zoo, the Parque de las Leyendas. A few weeks later, she was also surprised to discover that there was a US$14-million discrepancy in the ministry budget, including more than US$140,000 for 'two giraffes and two rhinoceroses'. These had apparently been ordered by her predecessor, Luisa María Cuculiza, known as 'La Cuculiza', but had never arrived at the zoo. When ministry officials asked the firm that was supposed to have captured the animals in Africa and delivered them to Peru what had happened to them, they were told amidst peals of laughter that 'their employees were still out on safari hunting for them'.

Alan García, the candidate for APRA. Until only a few months before the April 2001 poll, it had been unclear whether he would legally be allowed to stand, but he returned triumphantly to Peru and began to campaign forcefully on a platform of economic growth and redistribution of wealth.

In the end, it was Toledo and García who emerged as the two candidates to go forward to a second round of voting on 3 June. Although for a while it looked as though García might score an improbable victory, the final count gave Toledo some 53 per cent of the vote. His *Peru Possible* party also won 47 seats in Congress, which, thanks to a reform brought in by the Paniagua administration, was elected on a local basis rather than from national party lists; the idea was to create greater participation and sense of responsibility.

After the experience of so many years of illegal, manipulative government, Alejandro Toledo's election created immense expectations. All those groups and sectors in Peruvian society who had opposed the regime of Fujimori and Montesinos hoped that finally they would get an honest and responsible government, which would attend to the pressing needs of a society with increasing levels of poverty, a chronic sense of social exclusion that had been deepened by the manoeuvres of the previous regime, and, above all, a desire for an end to corruption in public life. In 2001, a survey carried out as part of the National Anti-Corruption Campaign found that 87 per cent of Peruvians in 2001 still identified corruption as the main stumbling block to a properly functioning democracy in their country.

5
Picking Up the Pieces

Despite fears that Fujimori's abrupt renunciation of power in November 2000 could lead to a military coup, Peru's politicians for once acted swiftly and decisively. Valentín Paniagua was sworn in as caretaker president within one day of Fujimori's faxed resignation. A veteran politician in his sixties, Paniagua represented the honest, democratic tradition of the political parties (in his case, *Acción Popular*) that Fujimori and Montesinos had done so much to undermine during their decade in power.

Javier Pérez de Cuellar's return to a position of influence after having lost badly to Fujimori in the 1995 elections was welcomed both in Peru and abroad. He in turn brought in a cabinet of 'notables' from political parties, NGOs and civil society. The caretaker government set itself the task of beginning to pick up the pieces after all that the collapse of the Fujimori regime had revealed about the grave failings of the Peruvian state.

In some areas, the caretaker government decided not to make a decisive break with the Fujimori era. They continued with similar economic policies, trying to achieve a fiscal balance and respecting payments of the foreign debt. They saw their main aim as paving the way for free and fair elections in April 2001, while at the same time starting to clear the state institutions of all those who had supported Fujimori and Montesinos in their criminal activities.

Some observers criticised the fact that they not only accepted Fujimori's timetable for the new ballot, but also did not seize the opportunity to reform the 1992 Constitution, which Fujimori had drawn up to cement his position in power. Instead, the Paniagua government drew up a proposal for the bases of constitutional reform, to be implemented by whichever political force emerged as victors from the April 2001 elections.

In the few months it was in power, the Paniagua administration did make determined attempts to rescue Peru from what has been called its 'spiritual bankruptcy'. Perhaps the most important measure in this respect was the establishment of a Truth and Reconciliation Commission to investigate the killings and human rights abuses that had taken place between 1980 and 2000, the years when the armed forces and guerrilla groups were involved in a struggle that claimed many thousands of innocent lives.

The caretaker government also ordered the public showing of the 'Vladivideos', and the prosecution of all those who appeared on the basis of that evidence to have a case to answer. In addition, a series of measures was put before Congress which together made up what became known as the 'anti-corruption' system. A special anti-corruption prosecutor (José Ugaz) was appointed, who began to sift through all the evidence of corruption and other abuses in order to build up cases that could be brought before the courts. The new government rightly felt that indignation or condemnation in the press was not enough: it was important to show that Fujimori, Montesinos and their accomplices had committed specific crimes, for which they could be brought to book.

As a result, for the first time in Peruvian history, generals, judges, ministers, well-known business figures and media bosses were arrested and put on trial. In Congress the Waisman Commission was set up to investigate the extent of the Fujimori-Montesinos criminal activities. The commission soon discovered foreign bank accounts linked to Montesinos totalling at least US$200 million, although this was thought to be only a small proportion of the amount he had siphoned off from the Peruvian state. The Paniagua team also proposed far-reaching reforms of the justice system and the police; the latter have begun by fits and starts, but the former have not yet been acted upon.

President Paniagua also considered it vital to uphold Peru's democratic traditions by respecting the election timetable already agreed. He and his cabinet stepped down after the successful organisation of the April 2001 elections. In July 2001, the third president in a year took up residence in Lima's presidential palace. This time there were none of the protests that had greeted Alberto Fujimori's attempts to prolong his rule into the new millennium. Alejandro Toledo was recognised inside Peru and internationally as having won free and fair elections, and he was enthusiastically welcomed by all those who had supported him for the previous two years.

Toledo was widely seen as the country's best hope to lead the healing of a divided and disillusioned society. He was the first elected president from Peru's indigenous minority: his climb from being a poor child from a family of sixteen in the fishing port of Chimbote to studying economics at Stanford University in the United States and becoming a World Bank official was a real rags-to-riches story. His election slogan had been 'mas trabajo', but although unemployment and the reduction of poverty were seen as priorities for his government, he was also expected to continue the overhaul of the state and its institutions set in train during the Paniagua transitional government.

One of the main tasks was to ensure that those found responsible for crimes during the Fujimori–Montesinos were put on trial. The former president himself appeared to be quite secure in Japan, since that country had recognised his Japanese nationality, as the child of two parents born in Japan. The Japanese authorities paid little attention to the requests for extradition formally presented to them in 2004, despite the fact that these included allegations of involvement in the setting-up of death squads in cases such as that of Barrios Altos and La Cantuta. Not only that, but Fujimori was allowed to come and go freely in Tokyo, and to express his political opinions in interviews and on his own website, despite the fact that he had been barred from political life in Peru for ten years.

After his brief escapes to Panama and Venezuela, Vladimiro Montesinos was not so lucky. On his return to Peru and jail in June 2001, a team of special prosecutors worked on building up evidence in more than 60 cases against him. To the dismay of many Peruvians, especially in the human rights sector, the prosecutors began with the less complicated accusations, which they felt could be pursued with more chance of rapid success, and left the more serious charges of organising death squads and other gross human rights violations until later.

Montesinos' first public appearance in many months took place in February 2002, when he was brought face-to-face with Alberto Kouri (the man shown being bribed in the first of the 'Vladivideos' to surface). This was to set the tone for all the subsequent hearings. It took place in a small, plain court-room in the spick and span naval base in Callao. Fifty or so journalists were kept well to the rear of the court while the three judges filed in. The judges looked nervous and uneasy about the proceedings, particularly when their microphones did not seem to work. Alberto Kouri was led in and sat down in a chair facing the judges' bench. He was asked several questions, and then Montesinos himself was led in. This produced a stampede from the TV and press photographers, all of them desperate to get the best shots of Peru's most wanted man.

Montesinos looked extremely cool, in one of his trademark Dior shirts, as he sat down and answered the judges' questions to confirm his identity. But as soon as the prosecution began to put more questions to him about Kouri and what had happened between them, he started shouting that he did not recognise the court's authority to judge him. He also complained that since he was being held in solitary confinement, he could not consult his lawyers, and could not therefore conduct his own defence properly. At this, the session was suspended, and Montesinos was taken back – at huge expense, with helicopters, motorcade and an army escort – to his prison cell.

Gradually, however, the prosecution made headway in this and other cases. By the end of 2004 Montesinos had been sentenced to 15 years' imprisonment, while many of the more serious charges, including arms trafficking and grave human rights violations, were still waiting to be heard. He has never expressed anything but contempt for the trials. At one point in 2004, during a hearing involving several 'gutter press' editors, TV cameras even caught him writing out what he wanted the papers to use as their headlines for the next day's news.

In addition to Montesinos, by the end of 2003 another 36 people had been tried and sentenced for corruption or similar charges during the decade of rule by the 'Siamese twins'. More than 1,400 people, many of them top-ranking members of the armed forces, the police and the judiciary, had been charged, and as many as 96 foreign bank accounts and 400 properties seized by the authorities. But the most complicated cases involving Montesinos and the armed forces – the accusations of running arms to the Colombian FARC guerrillas and the organisation of death squads, which involves the former army commander-in-chief General Nicolás de Bari Hermoza Ríos – have yet to be fully presented.

In addition to these prosecutions, the Toledo administration endorsed the work of the Truth and Reconciliation Commission, set up by Paniagua to investigate the allegations of human rights abuses committed during the 'years of violence'. Despite resistance from the military members of the Paniagua government, ministers from a human rights background pushed for this to be as wide-ranging as possible, ignoring any earlier amnesties. And although President Paniagua was apparently reluctant to allow the investigations to cover the period when his *Acción Popular* party was in power, it was eventually decided that the period covered should be from 1980, when *Sendero Luminoso* declared its war on the Peruvian state, right up to the time when Fujimori fled the country.

The 12 members of the commission, as ratified by President Toledo, were deliberately chosen from among prominent non-politicians. They included members of different churches, human rights workers, and legal experts. The chairman was Salomon Lerner, the rector of Lima's Catholic University. He insisted that compiling the report on past human rights abuses was only the first part of the commission's task. In order to prevent any similar atrocities happening in the future, he argued that its findings and recommendations should be taught in schools, and used as a tool for reforming all state institutions. He also insisted that while finding out the truth about the violence was a public duty, the question of reconciliation should be left to individual consciences.

Once the commission's mandate had been confirmed by President Toledo, it set to work gathering evidence on the abuses committed. Commission members visited some 530 districts in every part of Peru. One innovative aspect was the holding of public sessions where ordinary Peruvians could recount their experiences of the violence openly and without fear of reprisal. These public meetings were held throughout the regions, and were vital for changing the image of the state from that of a distant, repressive entity to one that actually listened and responded to ordinary Peruvians' complaints.

Between September 2001 and the beginning of 2003, the Commission collected 17,000 individual testimonies concerning alleged human rights abuses. They were also able to interview prominent politicians involved in creating the anti-subversion policies, such as former president Alan García, as well as retired military officers. They even managed to interview Abimael Guzmán, the founder of *Sendero Luminoso*, no fewer than 17 times.

The Truth and Reconciliation Commission presented its report in August 2003. In nine volumes – almost three thousand pages altogether – the report gave details of the atrocities, murders, kidnappings and other human rights violations committed by all sides. The number of Peruvians estimated to have been killed in 20 years of political violence was put at some 69,000 (twice as high as had been previously thought). Some 85 per cent were inhabitants of Ayacucho and neighbouring highland provinces, the poorest areas in the country. Three out of four of those who died had Quechua or another indigenous language as their mother tongue, reflecting the huge divide in Peruvian society, with people left at the margins for centuries suffering violence yet again, at the hands of either the state or political activists supposedly fighting on their behalf.

One major difference between the Peruvian commission's report and that of similar initiatives in Latin America (Argentina, Chile and Guatemala) was that in Peru more than half (an estimated 54 per cent) of the abuses catalogued were carried out by the insurgent groups rather than agents of the state. At the same time, however, the commission dismissed the armed forces' claim that the violations they were responsible for had simply been 'excesses' committed by a few individuals. The report clearly accuses the state of committing murder, torture and human rights violations as part of a systematic response to the insurgent threat.

In its recommendations, the commission calls for all those identified as being responsible for human rights crimes to be brought to justice, and identifies some 150 people (of whom 42 were part of the state apparatus) against whom there could be sufficient evidence to start legal proceedings. It also suggests that symbolic reparations be made, such as the establishment of specific sites of remembrance, acts of recognition for those wrongfully imprisoned, and an explicit apology from the Peruvian state for the wrongs that it inflicted on thousands of its own citizens.

At the same time, the commission's report places great emphasis on the institutional changes needed to ensure that the violent civil conflict that occasioned the human rights violations can never happen again in Peru. The report calls for the social inclusion of poor, indigenous peasants by improving police and justice systems, improving access to justice, and making democracy meaningful at the local level. Among the institutional reforms it recommends are civilian control of the ministry of defence, modernisation of the police force, and strengthening judicial autonomy. The report also calls for reforms to the education system to try to wipe out illiteracy in the poorest areas of Peru and to increase respect for ethnic and cultural diversity.

It can be seen that the commission saw its role as much broader than that of uncovering the facts of what had happened in the years of civil conflict between 1980 and 2000. As the chairman, Salomon Lerner, has written:

The Truth and Reconciliation Commission understood that its task was not just to recount the facts of what had taken place, but also to interpret them in order to disclose their true significance for the history of our country. A moral lesson lies hidden in the mass of facts and in those that still have to be revealed: a narrative that speaks of resentment and contempt, of confusion and ignorance, of arrogance and humiliation, a narrative of profound social exclusion. Without this narrative, the history of contemporary Peru – and perhaps that of Latin America – is incomplete.[1]

Peruvian society greeted the report with only lukewarm praise when its nine volumes were handed to President Alejandro Toledo on 28 August 2003. Criticisms were levelled that it was too 'political', and the past links of some commission members to left-wing organisations were used in some quarters to dismiss it as being 'partial' – especially as the report described a lot of the violence that took place in the first half of the 1980s, when President Belaúnde Terry was in office. State violence tended to be clandestine in this period, and such exposure further tarnishes the country's democratic image. Others claimed that too much money had been spent on the commission, or that the methodology used to estimate the number of victims of the violence was flawed.

On 21 November 2003, President Toledo apologised on behalf of the Peruvian state for the wrongs that had been done to many thousands of ordinary Peruvians, and promised increased spending, of some 2.8 billion soles (approximately US$800 million), in Ayacucho and the other highland provinces. He also ordered the State Prosecutor's Office to pursue cases against all those accused of human rights violations.

In addition to these attempts to deal with injustices from the past, there was tremendous pressure from popular groups, NGOs and politicians to instigate thoroughgoing reform of almost all state institutions in order to prevent the abuses of the Fujimori–Montesinos era ever happening again. These initiatives focused above all on those sectors where ordinary citizens come into direct contact with the state: the judiciary, the armed forces, and the police. President Toledo committed himself to these reforms by signing the National Agreement of 2001, an attempt to continue the consensus gained in the overthrow of Fujimori and the during the months of transitional government.

Under Fujimori, the judiciary had lost all semblance of being an independent institution capable of upholding the rule of law and of opposing the executive where necessary. Many of Peru's leading judges had appeared in the infamous 'Vladivideos', and a large majority of Peruvians (some 84 per cent, according to a 2002 survey) regarded them as openly corrupt. As in many other areas however, the promised reforms of the system have been limited and slow to be put into practice. New appointments to the Supreme Court have been blocked, while at lower levels many judges from the Fujimori era appear to have carried on exactly as before.

By 2005 it was clear that the Toledo government had little political will to push through any far-reaching reform of the judicial system. The questions of the jurisdiction of military courts, increasing access to justice for poor and excluded groups, and making all levels of justice transparent and accountable had simply not been addressed. A plan put forward by the Special Commission for the Integral Reform of the Justice System (CERIAJUS) in June 2004 appeared to have made little progress.

The armed forces were another sector that had lost all prestige, owing to their involvement both in the human rights violations of the anti-subversive struggle and in the crimes of the Fujimori–Montesinos regime. Most Peruvians were horrified at the way Montesinos had worked hand-in-glove with them as the secret centre of power in Peru, and disgusted at their participation in so many corrupt scandals aimed solely at lining their own pockets. In 2000–2001, the moral credibility of the Peruvian armed forces as defenders of 'national sovereignty' was zero. Many of the highest-ranking officers were jailed to await charges arising out their complicity with Montesinos; others were pensioned off.

Apart from this, the most important initiative in this area brought in by President Toledo was the first ever appointment of a civilian as minister of defence. Another commission was set up, this time to investigate how the armed forces needed to be changed in order to bring them up to date, and to make them more responsive to the needs of a democratic state. This commission insisted upon building of a civilian ministry of defence, which would control the armed forces and define its role, rather than the other way round. It also emphasised the need to make the armed forces more professional, and to ensure that there was a proper separation of its duties from those of the police.

Between 2001 and 2003, some progress was made with these reforms, despite the reluctance of the armed forces, and difficulties in getting the measures through Congress. Then, in December 2003, defence minister Aurelio Loret de Mola resigned. He was replaced by the army commander-in-chief, General Roberto Chiabra. In this way, civilian control over the reforms was lost, and the armed forces recovered an almost free hand in conducting their own affairs, including their relations with the government.

A third area that the transitional government and leaders in the anti-corruption drive considered essential to reform was the Peruvian police force. Poorly paid, open to corruption, and rarely independent of the political grouping in power, the police were the representatives of the state who most often came into contact with ordinary citizens, and were therefore its most obvious symbol.

In 2001, yet another commission was set up, including representatives of NGOs as well as interior ministry officials and the police themselves. Their report identified the major problems in the police as corruption, political influence, poor conditions of service, and the breakdown of trust between the police force and the community it was designed to serve.

In 2002, Interior Minister Fernando Rospigliosi and his team set about implementing the suggested reforms. The idea of a neighbourhood police force was emphasised. The team was concerned with *seguridad ciudadana* – trying to get ordinary citizens to trust the police, to feel secure and not threatened by them. A clear distinction was made between this police force and the special forces charged with keeping public order, whether in demonstrations or in fighting subversive attacks. An accelerated training programme was brought in, with the aim of renewing the police personnel, and many of the highest-ranking officers who had been in post during the Fujimori years were dismissed.

At the same time, a great effort was made to improve the position of the ordinary policeman. Salaries and pension rights were improved, and a campaign 'A la policia se la respeta' ('Show respect for the police') was started in order to try to improve relations with the community. A police ombudsman was appointed to deal with complaints within the police about ill-treatment and other abuses: in 2002 alone, there were some 6,000 requests to investigate individual complaints.

The row caused by the decision to give the police force a new image by buying new uniforms immediately demonstrated the pressures involved in trying to change old, corrupt habits. This was the first time that such an order (involving several million dollars) had been put out to tender. There were immediate protests from within the police, from politicians and from the previous suppliers – all of whom, it was suspected, had benefited from the less than transparent transactions that had been the previous way of doing business.

There were similar rows over attempts to make equally transparent the purchase of petrol for police patrol cars, and other important acquisitions. These concrete attempts to break the cycle of corruption, and the resistance they generated, showed how ingrained at all levels the system of kickbacks was.

As with the other attempted reforms, by the end of 2004 the efforts to change the police had all but ended. The office of the ombudsman was abolished, as were other internal control mechanisms. Civilian control also came to an end in 2005 when the director of the police, General Félix Murazzo, was appointed interior minister. The reforming impulse that had seemed so strong in 2001 was lost, thanks to political prevarication and indecision under President Toledo.

Beyond these areas of reform, the experiences of the Fujimori era led to calls for a radical overhaul of the political system itself. Fujimori had been able to install himself successfully because of the lack of trust the vast majority of Peruvians felt towards the traditional political parties, which were seen as venal, inept and almost entirely self-seeking, only interested in people when it was time to vote.

After the 2001 elections, there was considerable debate in Congress and at grassroots level about what measures were needed to consolidate party democracy in Peru. One initiative, put into practice in late 2002, was the direct election of 25 new regional presidents. This was part of an effort to make politics more relevant to ordinary citizens by involving them at a local level; it is too early to say whether it has been successful or not. In the event, the ruling Peru Posible party won only 11 per cent of the votes, whereas Alan García's APRA won control of 12 regions. The unfortunate consequence of this was that the central government felt itself threatened by the new structures, and proved reluctant to transfer real power and resources to the regions.

On 1 October 2003, a new Law on Political Parties was unanimously adopted by Congress. This aimed to tighten up the rules for the registration of political parties and to encourage efforts to make these parties more accountable in terms of funding and the selection of their leaders and candidates. The effects of these changes can be seen in the 2006 elections and beyond that, although several of the parties have actively responded to the new provisions.

In general, the problem for building a viable democracy in Peru based on democratic political party rule is that the consensus achieved to get rid of Fujimori and Montesinos has not lasted. For many reasons – self interest, lack of leadership, internal contradictions – the parties have gone back to fighting for their quota of power and privilege, and seem to have lost sight of citizens' demand for a complete overhaul of the political system. As former education minister Nicolás Lynch has said, a majority of Peruvians see 'politics as politicians fighting among themselves. This distancing of citizens and their representatives, and the constant quarrelling of the latter, have led to a climate of despair among the population, which could eventually create the conditions for a popular revolt that the political parties could not control or influence.'[2]

Peruvians wanted an end to the authoritarianism of Fujimori and Montesinos, but they did not want simply to return to the political chicanery of weak parties dominated by an executive and its cronies, the old habits of corruption and lack

GASTON GARATEA, a member of the Truth and Reconciliation Commission, describes what happened when they accompanied forensic experts to dig up a mass grave of people killed in the 1980s in remote village of Quispillata. (More than 4,000 illegal burial sites were identified by the TRC throughout Peru.)

'It was known more or less where the mass grave was, and who might be buried there. The widows and other relatives crowded round. I was very impressed by the scientific way that the members of the Peruvian Institute of Forensic Archaeology (IPAF) used all the evidence they found to establish that eight bodies had been buried, and the way they found pieces of material and other clues which would help identify the dead. One of the women present suddenly recognised a belt and shouted: "I wove that belt for my husband."

'And of course all the people in the village were filled with grief; they were reliving what had happened as if it were yesterday. We held a mass in Quechua, then all the villagers organised a proper burial for the victims of the violence. It was very moving to hear the village authorities speak of how these people had been killed and buried like dogs, and how now they could be given a proper burial and given their dignity back. The bodies were placed in coffins, and everybody paraded round the village square, then each of the dead was taken to their own home, where there was a wake, and they were reburied the next day. And I felt that thanks to all this process, not only could the dead rest in peace, but the living could too.'

of representation that has too often characterised Peruvian politics in the 20th century. As Claude Auroi has written, the Fujimori–Montesinos phenomenon threw up difficult questions for all Peruvians:

how could such a lack of morality not only happen but take root? Did the corrupt practices really only happen after pressure, threats, videos? Or did they spread through a social body that was already worm-eaten, rotten, in a state of decomposition? If that were the case, those in power only took advantage of a generalised moral situation. Without doubt one day the Montesinos case will be seen as revealing the deep-seated ills of traditional Peruvian society.[3]

It is only since 1980, when people who could not read or write were given the vote, that fully democratic rule has been possible in Peru. The challenge now is not to return to the structures that were in place before Fujimori and Montesinos and their followers subverted the state for their own ends. Instead, a truly democratic alternative needs to be built. Many of the ideas and proposals put forward in the heady moments of 2000–2001 have since been shelved or at best partially implemented. At the same time, thanks to the struggle of the past six years, Peruvians at all levels of society have learnt that they do have a voice, that they can organise to bring about significant political change, and that no political force, however authoritarian or corrupt, can take them for granted.

In their efforts to have Alberto Fujimori extradited from Japan and Chile, the Peruvian judicial authorities have presented six cases they wish to see the former president answer. These are his involvement in the killings of Barrios Altos and La Cantuta; the use of the national intelligence headquarters ('El Pentagonito') as a torture centre; abuses committed during the 'palace coup' in 1992; aiding and abetting Vladimiro Montesinos' escape from Peru; the use of emergency decress to purchase MIG-29s and Sukhoi-25 planes; and the use of government funds for the purchase of the CCN Cable News Channel. As well as these six, Fujimori faces a further 23 cases, ranging from involvement in the death of the trade union leader Pedro Huilca to paying the astrologer Faisal to start a slander campaign against opposition politicians.

Notes

1. Peru Support Group, *Truth and Reconciliation*, London, 2004, pp. 2–3.
2. Nicolás Lynch, in Claude Auroi and Sandra Bossio (eds), *A Donde Va el Perú?*, Institut Universitaire d'Etudes du Développement, Cuzco, 2002, p. 31.
3. Claude Auroi, in ibid., p. 12.

Bibliography

APRODEH Peru, *El reto de la verdad y la justicia*, Lima, 2001.

Auroi, Claude and Bossio, Sandra, *A Donde Va el Perú?* Institut Universitaire d'Etudes du Développement, Cuzco, 2002.

Bowen, Sally, *The Fujimori File*, Peru Monitor, Lima, 2000.

Bowen, Sally and Holligan, Jane, *The Imperfect Spy: The Many Lives of Vladimiro Montesinos*, Peisa, Lima, 2003.

Congreso de la República del Perú, *Informe final de la comisión especial de la investigación sobre los delitos cometidos entre 1990–2000*, Lima, 2002.

Crabtree, John, *Peru*, Oxfam Country Profile, Oxford, 2002.

Crabtree, John and Thomas, Jim, *Fujimori's Peru: The Political Economy*, University of London Institute of Latin American Studies, London, 1998.

Dammert, Manuel, *Fujimori–Montesinos, El estado mafioso*, Ediciones El Virrey, Lima, 2001.

De Soto, Hernando, *El otro sendero*, Instituto Libertad y Democracia, Lima, 1987.

Fowks, Jacqueline, *Suma y resta de la realidad*, Fundación Friedrich Ebert, Lima, 2000.

Graham, Carol and Pettinato, Stefano, 'Assessing hardship and happiness: Mobility trends and expectations in the new market economies', Center on Social and Economic Dynamics Working Paper Series no. 7, Brookings Institution, Washington, DC, October 1999.

Jochamowitz, Luis, *Ciudadano Fujimori*, Peisa, Lima, 1993.

Manzetti, Luigi, *Privatization South American Style,* Oxford University Press, Oxford, 2000.

Ministerio de Justicia del Perú, *Un Perú sin corrupción*, Lima, 2000.

Oppenheimer, Andres, *Ojos vendados: Estados Unidos y el negocio de la corrupción en América Latina*, Editorial Sudamericana, Buenos Aires, 2001.

Peña, Saúl, *Psicoanálisis de la corrupción*, Peisa, Lima, 2003.

Peru Support Group, *Peru: Democracy at the Crossroads*, London, 2000.

Peru Support Group, *The Findings of Peru's Truth and Reconciliation Commission*, London, 2004.

Proética, *Primera conferencia nacional anticorrupción*, Proética, Lima, 2001.

Rospigliosi, Fernando, *El arte del engaño*, Productos Paraíso del Perú, Lima, 2000.

Shakespeare, Nicholas, *The Dancer Upstairs*, Harvill Press, London, 1995.

Simpson, John, *In the Forests of the Night*, Hutchinson, London, 1993.

Starn, O., I. Degregori and Kirk, R. (eds), *The Peru Reader*, Duke University Press, 1995.

Strong, Simon, *Sendero Luminoso: The World's Deadliest Revolutionary Force*, HarperCollins, London, 1992.

Tulchin, Joseph S. and Espach, Ralph H. (eds), *Combating Corruption in Latin America*, Johns Hopkins University Press, Baltimore, 2000.

Tulchin, Joseph S. and Bland, Gary (eds), *Peru in Crisis: Dictatorship or Democracy*, Woodrow Wilson Center Current Studies on Latin America, 1994.

Vargas Llosa, Mario, *A Fish in the Water*, Faber and Faber, London, 1994.

Wiener, Raúl E, *El Reeleccionista*, Lima, 1998.

Wilkinson, R., *Peru: Terrorism, Torture, and Human Rights*, Parliamentary Human Rights Group, London, 1996.

Youngers, Coletta, *Deconstructing Democracy: Peru under Fujimori*, Washington Office on Latin America, Washington, 2000.

www.ingramcontent.com/pod-product-compliance
Lightning Source LLC
Chambersburg PA
CBHW051029030426
42336CB00015B/2792